新丝路“中文＋职业技能”系列教材委员会
（中文＋汽车服务工程技术）

新丝路"中文+职业技能"系列教材
New Silk Road "Chinese + Vocational Skills" Series

中文+汽车服务工程技术
Chinese + Automotive Service Engineering Technology

高级 Advanced

新丝路"中文+职业技能"系列教材编写委员会 编

北京语言大学出版社
BEIJING LANGUAGE AND CULTURE UNIVERSITY PRESS

图书在版编目（CIP）数据

中文＋汽车服务工程技术．高级／新丝路“中文＋职业技能”系列教材编写委员会编．-- 北京：北京语言大学出版社，2024. 7. -- ISBN 978-7-5619-6570-2

Ⅰ. H195.4; F407.471.5

中国国家版本馆 CIP 数据核字第 202405K2F9 号

中文＋汽车服务工程技术（高级）

ZHONGWEN + QICHE FUWU GONGCHENG JISHU (GAOJI)

排版制作：北京创艺涵文化发展有限公司
责任印制：周　燚

出版发行：北京语言大学出版社
社　　址：北京市海淀区学院路 15 号，100083
网　　址：www.blcup.com
电子信箱：service@blcup.com
电　　话：编 辑 部　8610-82303647/3592/3724
国内发行　8610-82303650/3591/3648
海外发行　8610-82303365/3080/3668
北语书店　8610-82303653
网购咨询　8610-82303908
印　　刷：北京富资园科技发展有限公司

版　　次：2024 年 7 月第 1 版　　**印　　次**：2024 年 7 月第 1 次印刷
开　　本：889 毫米 × 1194 毫米　1/16　　**印　　张**：12
字　　数：194 千字
定　　价：98.00 元

PRINTED IN CHINA
凡有印装质量问题，本社负责调换。售后 QQ 号 1367565611，电话 010-82303590

编写说明

新丝路“中文＋职业技能”系列教材是把中文作为第二语言，结合专业和职业的专门用途、职业用途的中文教材，不是专业理论教材，不是一般意义的通用综合中文教材。本系列教材定位为职场生存中文教材、立体式技能型语言教材。教材研发的目标是既要满足学习者一般中文环境下的基本交际需求，又要满足学习者职业学习需求和职场工作需求。它和普通的国际中文教材的区别不在语法，而在词汇的专门化程度，在中文的用途、使用场合、应用范围。目前，专门用途、职业用途的中文教材在语言分类和研究成果上几近空白，本系列教材的成功研发开创了中文学习的新视野、新领域、新方向，将“中文＋职业技能＋X等级证书”真正融合，使学习者在学习中文的同时，也可通过实践掌握职业技能，从而获得X等级证书。

适用对象

本系列教材将适用对象定位为双零基础（零语言基础、零技能基础）的来华学习中文和先进技能的长期或者短期进修生，可满足初、中、高各层次专业课程的教学需要。教材亦可供海内外相关的培训课程及“走出去”的中资企业培训本土化员工使用。

结构规模

本系列教材采取专项语言技能与职业技能训练相结合的中文教学及教材编写模式。教材选择当前热门的物流管理、汽车服务工程技术、电子商务、机电一体化、计算机网络技术、酒店管理等六个专业，培养各专业急需急用的技术岗位人才。每个专业教材均包括初、中、高级三册。每一册都配有专业视频教学资源，还附有“视频脚本”“参考答案”等配套资源。

编写理念

本系列教材将词语进行分类，区分普通词语和专业词语，以通用语料为基础，以概念性、行为性词语为主，不脱离职场情境讨论分级，做到控制词汇量，控制工作场景，控制交流内容与方式，构建语义框架。将语言的分级和专业的分级科学地融合，是实现本系列教材成功编写的关键。

教材目标

语言技能目标：

初级阶段，能熟练掌握基础通用词语和职场的常用专业词语，能使用简短句子进行简单的生活及工作交流。中级阶段，能听懂工作场合简单的交谈与发言，明白大意，把握基本情况，能就工作中重要的话题用简单的话与人沟通。高级阶段，能听懂工作场合一般的交谈与发言，抓住主要内容和关键信息，使用基本交际策略与人交流、开展工作，能初步了解与交际活动相关的文化因素，掌握与交际有关的一般文化背景知识，能排除交际时遇到的文化障碍。交际能力层次的递进实现从初级的常规礼节、基本生活及工作的交流能力，到中级的简单的服务流程信息交流能力，最后达到高级的复杂信息的交流和特情处理的能力。

职业技能目标：

以满足岗位需求为目标，将遴选出的当前热门的专业工作岗位分为初、中、高三级。物流管理专业初、中、高级对应的岗位分别是物流员、物流经理、物流总监；汽车服务工程技术专业初、中、高级对应的岗位分别是汽车机电维修工、汽车服务顾问、技术总监；电子商务专业初、中、高级对应的岗位分别是电子商务运营助理、电子商务运营员、电子商务客服；机电一体化专业初、中、高级对应的岗位分别是机电操作工、机电调整工、机电维修工；计算机网络技术专业初、中、高级对应的岗位分别是宽带运维工程师、网络运维专员、网络管理员；酒店管理专业初、中、高级对应的岗位分别是前厅基层接待员、前厅主管、前厅经理。每个专业分解出三十个工作场景 / 任务，学习者在学习后能够全面掌握此岗位的概况及基本程序，实现语言学习和专业操作的双重目标。

编写原则

1. 语言知识技能与专业知识技能并进，满足当前热门的、急需急用的岗位需求。

2. 渐进分化，综合贯通，拆解难点，分而治之。

3. 语言知识与专业知识科学、高效复现，语言技能与专业技能螺旋式上升，职场情境、语义框架、本体输入方式相互配合。

4. 使用大量的图片和视频，实现专业知识和技能呈现形式可视化。

5. 强化专业岗位实操性技能。本系列教材配有专业技术教学的视频，突出展示专业岗位的实操性技能，语言学习难度与技能掌握难度的不匹配可通过实操性强的视频和实训环节来补充。

特色追求

本系列教材从初级最基础的语音知识学习和岗位认知开始，将“中文 + 职业技能”融入在工作场景对话中，把工作分解成一个个任务，用图片认知的方式解决专业词语的认知问题，用视频展示的方法解决学习者掌握中文词语与专业技能的不匹配问题，注重技能的实操性，注重"在做中学"。每一单元都设置了"学以致用"板块，目的不仅仅是解决本单元任务的词语认知问题，更是将学习的目标放在"能听""能用""能模仿说出"上。我们力争通过大量图片的使用和配套视频的展示，将教材打造成立体式、技能型语言教材，方便学习者能够更好地自主学习。

使用建议

1. 本系列教材每个专业分为初、中、高级三册，每册10单元，初级每单元建议8～10课时完成，中级10～12课时完成，高级12～14课时完成。

2. 教材注释和说明着力于简明扼要，注重实操性，注重听说技能培养，对于教材涉及的语法知识，教师可视情况予以细化和补充。

3. "单元实训"板块可以在课文和语言点学完之后作为课堂练习使用，建议2课时完成。教师要带着学习者按照实训步骤一步步完成，实训步骤不要求学习者能够看懂，读懂，重要的是教师要引领操作，实现学习者掌握专业技能的目标。

4. "单元小结"板块是对整个单元关键词语和核心内容的总结，对于这部分内容，教师要进行听说练习，以便更好地帮助学习者了解本单元的核心工作任务。

5. 教师上课时要充分利用教材设计的练习，引导学习者多听多练，听说结合，学做合一。

6. 教师要带着学习者熟练诵读课文，要求学习者把每课的关键词语和句子、课堂用语背诵下来。

特别感谢

感谢教育部中外语言交流合作中心将新丝路"中文＋职业技能"系列教材列为重点研发项目，为我们教材编写增添了动力和责任感。教材编写委员会负责整套教材的规划、设计与编写协调，并先后召开上百次讨论会，对每册教材的课文编写、体例安排、注释说明、练习设计、图片选择、视频制作等进行全方位的评估、讨论和审定。感谢编写委员会成员和所有编者高度的敬业精神、精益求精的编写态度，以及所投入的热情和精力、付出的心血与智慧。感谢关注本系列教材并贡献宝贵意见的国际中文教育教学界专家和全国各地的同人。

新丝路"中文＋职业技能"系列教材编写委员会

2023年4月

Compilation Instructions

The New Silk Road "Chinese + Vocational Skills" is a series of Chinese textbooks for specialized and vocational purposes that combine professional and vocational technologies with Chinese as a second language. Instead of being specialized theoretical textbooks, or comprehensive or universal Chinese textbooks in a general sense, this series is intended to be Chinese textbooks for career survival, and three-dimensional skills-based language textbooks. The textbooks are developed with a view to meeting students' basic communication needs in general Chinese environment, and their professional learning needs and workplace demands as well. They are different from ordinary Chinese textbooks for foreigners in the degree of specialization of vocabulary, in the purpose, usage occasion, and application scope of Chinese (not in grammar). At present, Chinese textbooks for specialized and vocational purposes are virtually non-existent in terms of language classification and research results, so the successful development of this series has opened up new horizons, new fields and new directions for Chinese learning, and virtually integrated "Chinese + Vocational Skills + X-Level Certificates", which enables students to practically master vocational skills and obtain X-level certificates while learning Chinese.

Applicable Targets

This series is targeted at long-term or short-term students who come to China to learn Chinese and advanced skills with zero language basis and zero skill basis, which can meet the teaching needs of the elementary, intermediate and advanced specialized courses. This series can also be used for relevant training courses at home and abroad and for Chinese-funded enterprises that "go global" to train local employees.

Structure and Scale

This series adopts a Chinese teaching and textbook compilation model combining special language skills and vocational skills training. The series includes the textbooks for six popular majors such as logistics management, automotive service engineering technology, e-commerce, mechatronics, computer networking technology, and hotel management to cultivate technical talents in urgent need. The textbooks for each major consist of the textbooks at the elementary, intermediate and advanced levels. Each textbook is equipped with professional video teaching resources, and "video scripts", "reference answers" and other supporting resources as well.

Compilation Concept

This series classifies the vocabulary into general vocabulary and specialized vocabulary. Based on the general vocabulary, it focuses on conceptual and behavioral words, not deviating from workplace situations, so as to control the vocabulary, work scenarios and content and means of communication, and build the semantic framework. The scientific integration of language classification and specialty classification is the key to the successful compilation of textbooks.

Textbook Objectives

Language Skill Objectives

For students at the elementary level, they are trained to be familiar with basic general vocabulary and common specialized vocabulary in the workplace, and be able to use short sentences for simple communication in life and at work. For those at the intermediate level, they are trained to understand simple conversations and speeches in the workplace, comprehend the main ideas, grasp the basic situations, and communicate with others in simple words on important topics at work. For those at the advanced level, they are trained to be able to understand general conversations and speeches in the workplace, grasp the main content and key information, use basic communication strategies to communicate with others and carry out the work, have a preliminary understanding of cultural factors related to communication activities, master the general communication-related cultural background knowledge, and overcome cultural barriers encountered during communication. The progression in level of communicative competence helps them to leap forward from routine etiquette, basic communication in life and at work at the elementary level, to simple information exchange of service processes at the intermediate level, and finally to complex information exchange and handling of special circumstances at the advanced level.

Vocational Skill Objectives

To meet job requirements at the elementary, intermediate and advanced levels, the professional positions that are most urgently needed overseas are selected. The positions corresponding to logistics management at the elementary, intermediate and advanced levels are logistics staff, logistics managers and logistics directors; the positions corresponding to automotive service engineering technology at the elementary, intermediate and advanced levels are automotive electromechanical maintenance staff, automotive service consultants and technical directors; the positions corresponding to e-commerce at the elementary, intermediate and advanced levels are electronic operation assistants, e-commerce operators and e-commerce customer service staff; the positions corresponding to mechatronics at the elementary, intermediate and advanced levels are mechanical and electrical operators, mechanical and electrical adjusters, and mechanical and electrical maintenance staff; the positions corresponding to computer networking technology at the elementary, intermediate and advanced levels are broadband operation and maintenance engineers, network operation and maintenance specialists, and network administrators; the positions corresponding to hotel management at the elementary, intermediate and advanced levels are lobby receptionists, lobby supervisors and lobby managers. Through 30 work scenarios/tasks set for each major, learners can fully grasp the general situations and basic procedures of the position after learning, and achieve the dual goals of language learning and professional operation.

Principles of Compilation

1. Language knowledge skills and professional knowledge skills go hand in hand to meet the demands of current popular and urgently needed job positions;

2. It makes progressive differentiation and comprehensive integration, breaking down, dividing and conquering difficult points;

3. Language knowledge and professional knowledge recur scientifically and efficiently, language skills and professional skills spiral upward, and the situational stage, semantic framework, and ontology input methods cooperate with each other;

4. Professional knowledge and skills are visualized, using a lot of pictures and videos;

5. It strengthens the practical skills in professional positions. This series of textbooks is equipped with videos of professional technical training, highlighting the practical skills for professional positions. It addresses the mismatch between the difficulty of language learning and that of mastering skills by supplementing with practical videos and practical training.

Characteristic Pursuit

Starting from the basic phonetic knowledge learning and job cognition at the elementary level, this series integrates "Chinese + Vocational Skills" into the working scene dialogues, breaking down the job into various tasks, solving lexical students' problems by means of picture cognition, solving the problem of the mismatch between students' mastery of Chinese vocabulary and professional skills by means of displaying videos, stressing the practicality of skills, and focusing on "learning by doing". Each unit has a "Practicing What You Have Learnt" module, which not only solves the problem of lexical cognition of this unit, but also takes "being able to comprehend", "being able to use" and "being able to imitate" as the learning objectives. We strive to use a large number of pictures and display supporting videos to build the textbooks into three-dimensional skills-based language teaching materials, so that learners can learn more independently.

Recommendations for Use

1. Each major of this series consists of three volumes at the elementary, intermediate, and advanced levels, with 10 units in each volume. For each unit, it is recommended to be completed in 8-10 class hours at the elementary level, 10-12 class hours at the intermediate level, and 12-14 class hours at the advanced level.

2. The notes and explanations in the textbooks focus on conciseness, practicality, and the training of listening and speaking skills. The grammar knowledge in the textbooks can be detailed and supplemented by teachers as the case may be.

3. "Unit Practical Training" module can be used as a classroom exercise after the texts and language points, preferably to be completed in two class hours. Teachers should guide students to complete the training tasks step by step. Students are not required to read and understand the training steps. It is important that teachers guide students to achieve the goal of mastering professional skills.

4. "Unit Summary" module summarizes the keywords and core content of the entire unit. Through listening and speaking exercises, this part can better help learners understand the core tasks of this unit.

5. Teachers should make full use of the exercises designed in the textbooks during class, and guide students to listen more and practice more, combine listening and speaking, and integrate learning with practice.

6. Teachers should guide students to proficiently read the texts aloud, asking them to recite the keywords, sentences and classroom expressions in each unit.

Acknowledgements

We are grateful to the Center for Language Education and Cooperation of the Ministry of Education for listing the New Silk Road "Chinese + Vocational Skills" series as a key research and development project, which adds motivation and a sense of responsibility to our textbook compilation. The Textbook Compilation Committee is responsible for the planning, design, compilation and coordination of the entire set of textbooks, and has held hundreds of seminars to conduct a comprehensive evaluation, discussion, examination and approval of text compilation, style arrangement, notes and explanations, exercise design, picture selection, and video production of each textbook. We are indebted to the members of the Compilation Committee and all compilers for their professional dedication, unwavering pursuit of perfection in the compilation, as well as their enthusiasm, hard work and wisdom. We are thankful to the experts in international Chinese language education and colleagues from all over the country who have kept a close eye on this series and contributed their valuable opinions.

Compilation Committee of New Silk Road "Chinese + Vocational Skills" Series

April 2023

rénwù jièshào

人物介绍

Introduction to Characters

shīfu
师傅
Master

xuétú túdi
学徒（徒弟）
Apprentice

wéixiūgōng
维修工
Maintenance Technician

jìshù zǒngjiān
技术总监
Technical Director

kèhù jīnglǐ
客户经理
Customer Manager

gùkè
顾客
Customer

语法术语及缩略形式参照表
Abbreviations of Grammar Terms

Grammar Terms in Chinese	Grammar Terms in Pinyin	Grammar Terms in English	Abbreviations
名词	míngcí	noun	n.
专有名词	zhuānyǒu míngcí	proper noun	pn.
代词	dàicí	pronoun	pron.
数词	shùcí	numeral	num.
量词	liàngcí	measure word	m.
数量词	shùliàngcí	quantifier	q.
动词	dòngcí	verb	v.
助动词	zhùdòngcí	auxiliary	aux.
形容词	xíngróngcí	adjective	adj.
副词	fùcí	adverb	adv.
介词	jiècí	preposition	prep.
连词	liáncí	conjunction	conj.
助词	zhùcí	particle	part.
拟声词	nǐshēngcí	onomatopoeia	onom.
叹词	tàncí	interjection	int.
前缀	qiánzhuì	prefix	pref.
后缀	hòuzhuì	suffix	suf.
成语	chéngyǔ	idiom	idm.
短语	duǎnyǔ	phrase	phr.
主语	zhǔyǔ	subject	S
谓语	wèiyǔ	predicate	P
宾语	bīnyǔ	object	O
定语	dìngyǔ	attributive	Attrib
状语	zhuàngyǔ	adverbial	Adverb
补语	bǔyǔ	complement	C

CONTENTS

目录

1 Gùzhàng zhěnduànyí gōngnéng
故障诊断仪功能
Functions of a Fault Diagnosis Instrument

gùzhàng zhěnduànyí dúqǔ shùjùliú de cāozuò liúchéng

故障 诊断仪读取数据流的操作 流程

The Operating Procedure of Using a Fault Diagnosis Instrument to Read the Data Flow

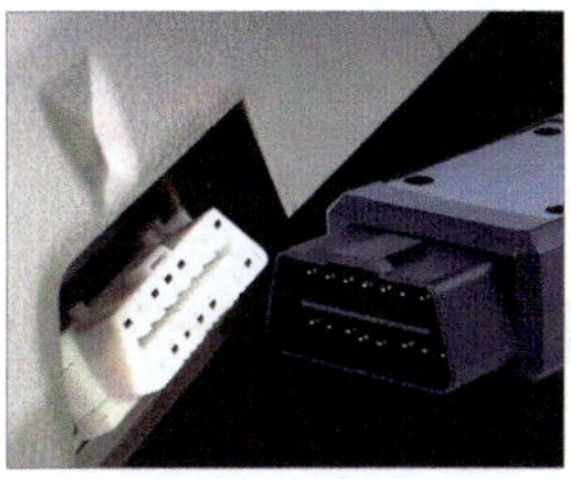

liánjiē gùzhàng zhěnduànyí

连接 故障 诊断仪

Connect the Fault Diagnosis Instrument

dǎkāi gùzhàng zhěnduànyí kāiguān

打开 故障 诊断仪 开关

Turn on the Switch of the Fault Diagnosis Instrument

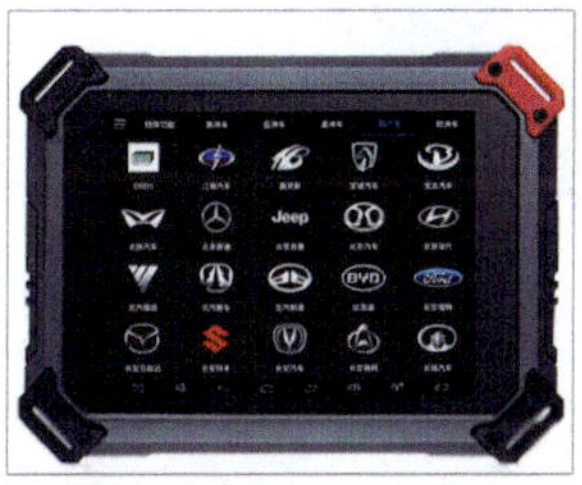

chákàn chēliàng xìnxī

查看 车辆 信息

Check the Vehicle Information

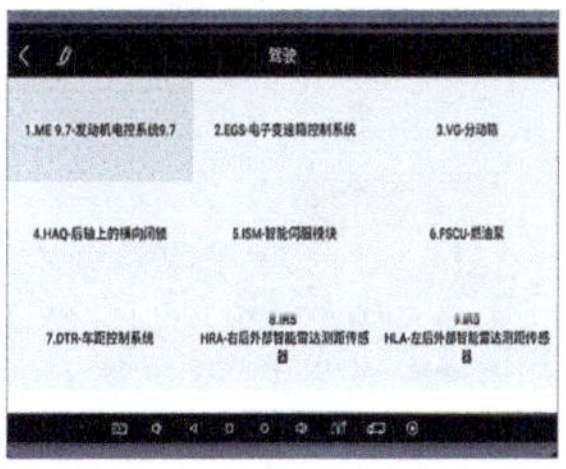

xuǎnzé cèshì xìtǒng

选择测试系统

Select the Test System

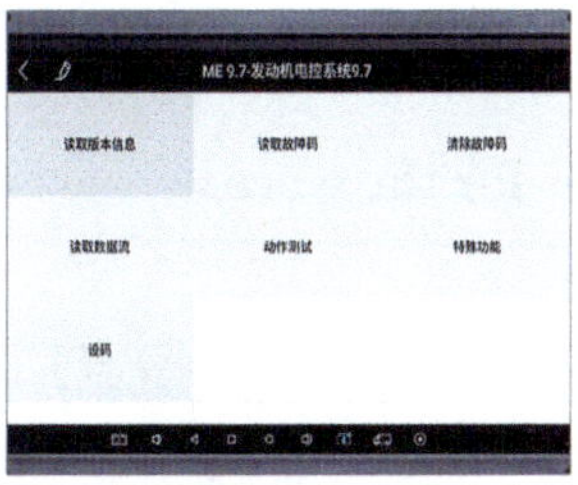

dúqǔ shùjùliú

读取数据流

Read the Data Flow

chákàn shùjù

查看数据

Check the Data

题解 Introduction

1. 学习内容：故障诊断仪的功能和使用方法，包括故障码的读取和解读。
   Learning content: The functions and usage methods of a fault diagnosis instrument, including reading and interpreting fault codes
2. 知识目标：学习使用故障诊断仪的关键词和常用句型，学习汉字的偏旁和结构，学写相关汉字。
   Knowledge objectives: To learn the keywords and common sentence patterns for the use of a fault diagnosis instrument, learn the radicals and structures of Chinese characters, and learn to write the related Chinese characters
3. 技能目标：掌握使用故障诊断仪读取故障码的操作方法。
   Skill objective: To master the method of using a fault diagnosis instrument to read fault codes

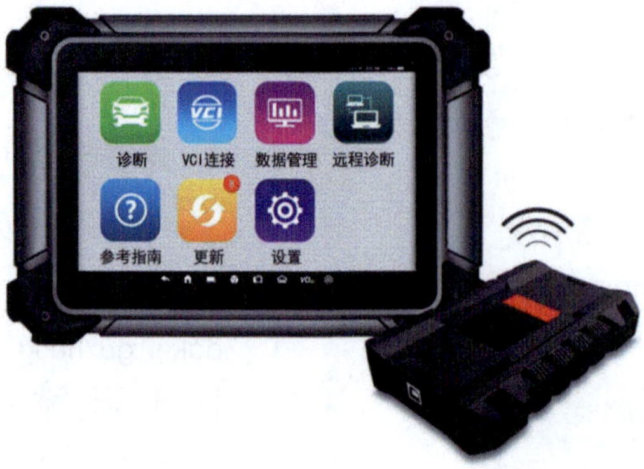

第一部分 Part 1

课文 Texts

一、热身 rèshēn Warm-up

1. 给词语选择对应的图片。**Choose the corresponding pictures for the words.**

A.

B.

C.

D.

gùzhàng zhěnduànyí
❶ 故障 诊断仪 ________________
fault diagnosis instrument

dì-èr dài chēzài zhěnduàn xìtǒng
❷ 第二代车载 诊断 系统（OBD-II）________________
on-board diagnostics II (OBD-II)

chēzài zhěnduàn chātóu
❸ 车载 诊断 插头________________
OBD connector

lányá mókuài
❹ 蓝牙模块________________
bluetooth module

2. 观看介绍 OBD-II 诊断接口的相关视频，将 OBD-II 诊断接口 16 个端子的序号与对应的诊断项目配对。**Watch the related video introducing the OBD-II diagnostic interface and match the serial numbers of the 16 pins of the OBD-II diagnostic interface with the corresponding diagnostic items.**

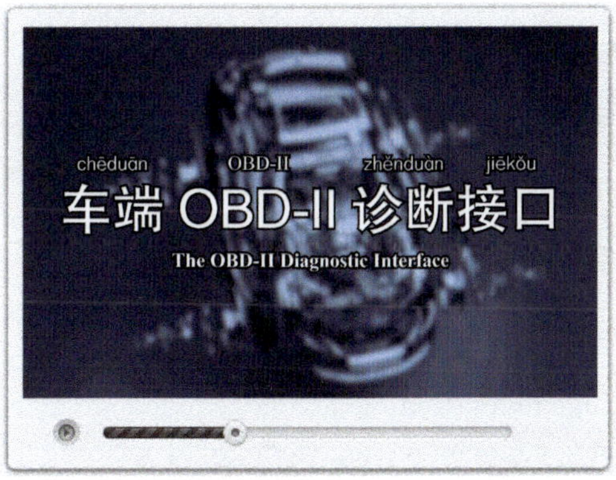

车端OBD-II诊断接口

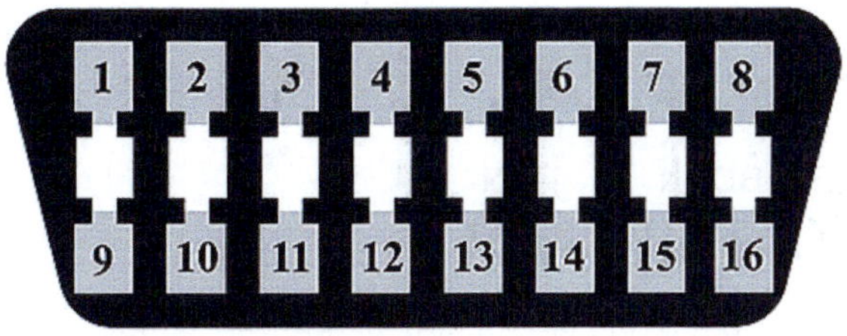

chǎngjiā zìdìngyì jiēkǒu
❶ 厂家 自定义接口________________、________________、________________、
manufacturer's custom interfaces

________________、________________、________________

SAEJ1850 zǒngxiàn
❷ SAEJ1850 总线（+）________________
SAE J1850 bus (+)

SAEJ1850 zǒngxiàn
、SAEJ1850 总线（−）________________
SAE J1850 bus (–)

chēshēn dātiě
❸ 车身 搭铁________________
body grounding

xìnhào dātiě
❹ 信号搭铁 ________________
signal grounding

❺ CAN-H ________________
CAN-H

CAN-L ________________
CAN-L

❻ K-line ________________
K-line

L-line ________________
L-line

chángdiàn
❼ 常电 ________________
constant current

二、课文 kèwén Texts

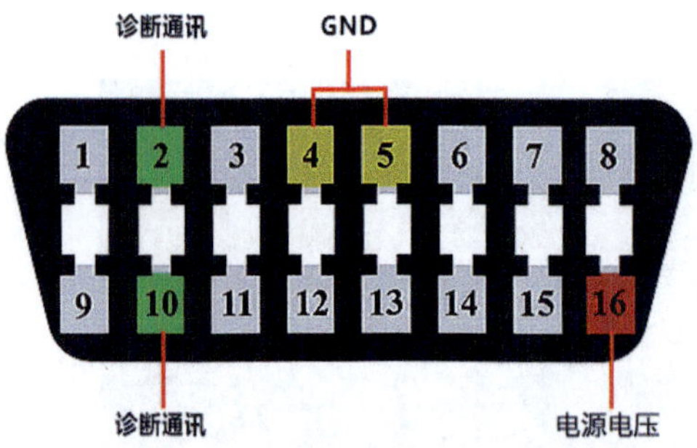

A 01-01

túdí: Shīfu, zhè liàng qìchē fādòngjī yùnxíng bù wěn, bù zhīdào chūle shénme gùzhàng.
徒弟：师傅，这 辆 汽车发动机 运行 不稳，不知道 出了什么 故障。

shīfu: Nǐ bǎ gùzhàng zhěnduànyí ná guolai, bǎ lányá mókuài jiērù qìchē dì-èr dài chēzài zhěnduàn xìtǒng (OBD-II) jiēkǒu.
师傅：你把 故障 诊断仪 拿过来，把蓝牙模块接入汽车第二代车载 诊断 系统（OBD-II）接口。

túdí: Měi liàng chē de chēzài zhěnduàn xìtǒng jiēkǒu dōu shì xiāngtóng de ma?
徒弟：每 辆 车的车载 诊断 系统 接口都 是 相同 的吗？

shīfu: Shìde, dōu shì guójì biāozhǔn jiēkǒu. Nǐ kàn zhège tú, zhěnduàn jiēkǒu yǒu 16 gè
师傅：是的，都是国际标准接口。你看这个图，诊断接口有16个
duānzǐ. Yǒu jǐ gè shì guīdìng jiēkǒu, qítā de shì chǎngshāng zìdìngyì jiēkǒu.
端子。有几个是规定接口，其他的是厂商自定义接口。

译文 yìwén Text in English

Apprentice: Master, the engine of this vehicle is running unsteadily. I don't know what the problem is.

Master: Bring the fault diagnosis instrument over and connect the bluetooth module to the OBD-II interface of the vehicle.

Apprentice: Is the OBD interface of each vehicle the same?

Master: Yes, they are internationally standardized interfaces. Look at this figure. The diagnostic interface has 16 pins. Some are specified interfaces, and others are manufacturer's custom interfaces.

普通词语 pǔtōng cíyǔ General Vocabulary

01-02

1.	稳	wěn	adj.	stable
2.	出	chū	v.	occur
3.	拿	ná	v.	bring
4.	每	měi	pron.	every
5.	相同	xiāngtóng	adj.	same
6.	这个	zhège	pron.	this

专业词语 zhuānyè cíyǔ Specialized Vocabulary

01-03

1.	运行	yùnxíng	v.	run, operate
2.	蓝牙模块	lányá mókuài	phr.	bluetooth module
3.	接入	jiērù	v.	access
4.	第二代车载诊断系统	dì-èr dài chēzài zhěnduàn xìtǒng	phr.	on-board diagnostics II (OBD-II)
5.	接口	jiēkǒu	n.	interface
6.	国际标准	guójì biāozhǔn	phr.	international standard
7.	诊断	zhěnduàn	v.	diagnose
8.	端子	duānzǐ	n.	pin, stitch
9.	规定接口	guīdìng jiēkǒu	phr.	specified interface
10.	厂商自定义接口	chǎngshāng zìdìngyì jiēkǒu	phr.	manufacturer's custom interface

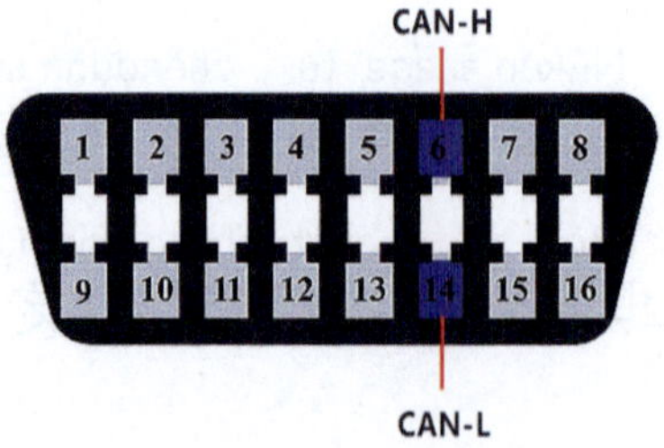

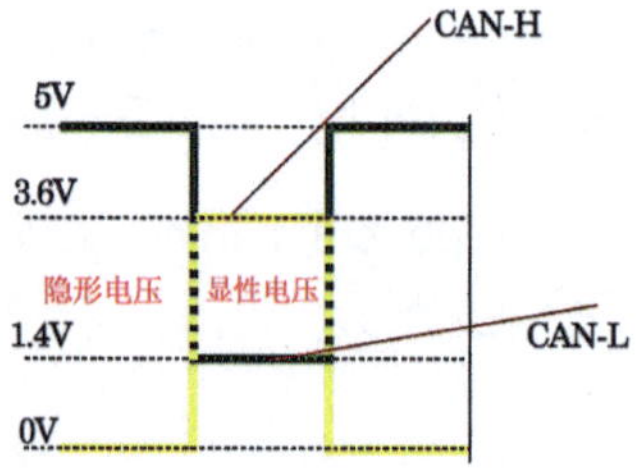

B 01-04

wéixiūgōng: Shīfu, xiànzài qìchē shang dàdū cǎiyòng kòngzhìqì júyù wǎngluò xìtǒng chuánshū shùjù ma?

维修工：师傅，现在汽车上大都采用控制器局域网络系统传输数据吗？

jìshù zǒngjiān: Shìde, dàbùfen chēliàng dōu shì tōngguò duānzǐ 6、duānzǐ 14 yǔ gùzhàng zhěnduànyí tōngxìn, tōngguò CAN-H、CAN-L liǎng gè CAN zǒngxiàn chuánshū shùjù. Rúguǒ CAN tōngxìn chūxiàn wèntí, gùzhàng zhěnduànyí shì wúfǎ dúqǔ chēliàng xìnxī de, zhěnggè chēliàng yě shì wúfǎ qǐdòng de.

技术总监：是的，大部分车辆都是通过端子6、端子14与故障诊断仪通信，通过CAN-H、CAN-L两个CAN总线传输数据。如果CAN通信出现问题，故障诊断仪是无法读取车辆信息的，整个车辆也是无法起动的。

wéixiūgōng: Nà wǒmen zěnme pànduàn shì bu shì CAN zǒngxiàn chūxiànle wèntí ne?

维修工：那我们怎么判断是不是CAN总线出现了问题呢？

jìshù zǒngjiān: Kěyǐ tōngguò shìbōqì dúqǔ CAN-H hé CAN-L de bōxíng lái pànduàn.

技术总监：可以通过示波器读取CAN-H和CAN-L的波形来判断。

译文 yìwén Text in English

Maintenance Technician: Master, is the CAN bus system mainly used in vehicles to transmit data today?

Technical Director: Yes. Most vehicles communicate with the fault diagnosis instrument through PIN 6 and PIN 14, and transmit data through two CAN buses (CAN-H and CAN-L). If there is a problem with CAN communication, the fault diagnosis instrument cannot read the vehicle information, and the vehicle cannot be started.

Maintenance Technician: Then how can we tell whether there is a problem with the CAN bus?

Technical Director: We can read the waveforms of CAN-H and CAN-L through an oscilloscope.

普通词语 pǔtōng cíyǔ General Vocabulary 01-05

1.	大都	dàdū	adv.	mostly, mainly

2.	大部分	dàbùfen	n.	most, majority
3.	如果	rúguǒ	conj.	if
4.	出现	chūxiàn	v.	appear
5.	无法	wúfǎ	v.	be unable (to do sth.)
6.	读取	dúqǔ	v.	read, get
7.	信息	xìnxī	n.	information
8.	怎么	zěnme	pron.	how
9.	判断	pànduàn	v.	judge, tell

专业词语 zhuānyè cíyǔ Specialized Vocabulary

01-06

1.	采用	cǎiyòng	v.	adopt
2.	控制器局域网络	kòngzhìqì júyù wǎngluò	phr.	Controller Area Network (CAN)
3.	传输	chuánshū	v.	transmit
4.	数据	shùjù	n.	data
5.	通信	tōngxìn	v.	communicate
6.	起动	qǐdòng	v.	start
7.	波形	bōxíng	n.	waveform

三、视听说 shì-tīng-shuō Viewing, Listening and Speaking

1. 观看介绍故障诊断仪数据流读取的视频，了解故障诊断仪的操作流程，并给操作流程排序。

Watch the video introducing the data flow reading of a fault diagnosis instrument, learn the operation process of using a fault diagnosis instrument, and rearrange the operation process.

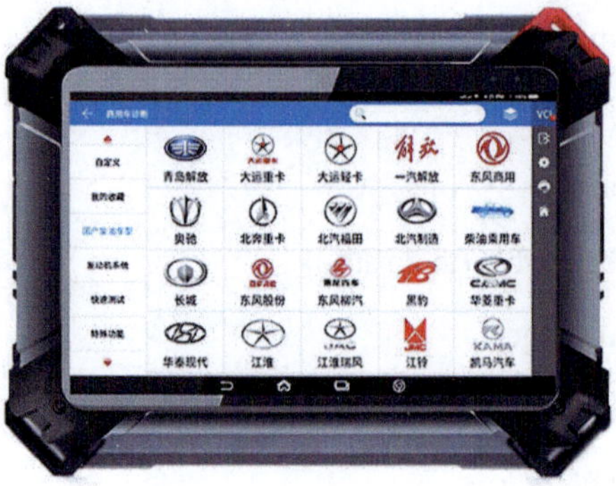

Chákàn chēliàng xìnxī, bìng zài càidānlán zhōng xuǎnzé chēxíng.
A. 查看 车辆 信息，并在菜单栏 中 选择 车型。
Check the vehicle information, and select the vehicle model in the menu bar.

Liánjiē chēliàng.
B. 连接 车辆。
Connect the vehicle.

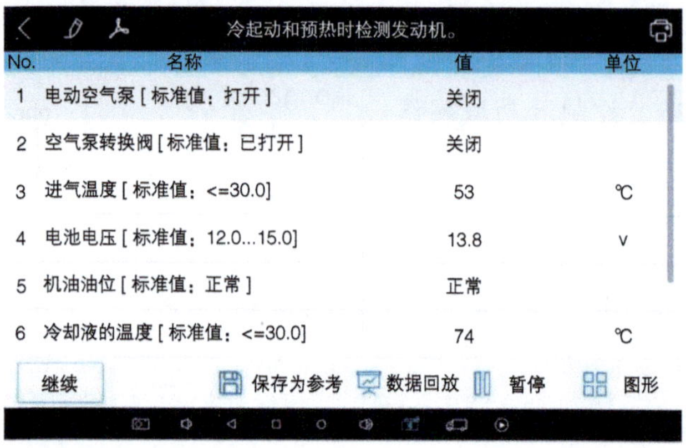

Chákàn shùjùliú.
C. 查看 数据流。
Check the data flow.

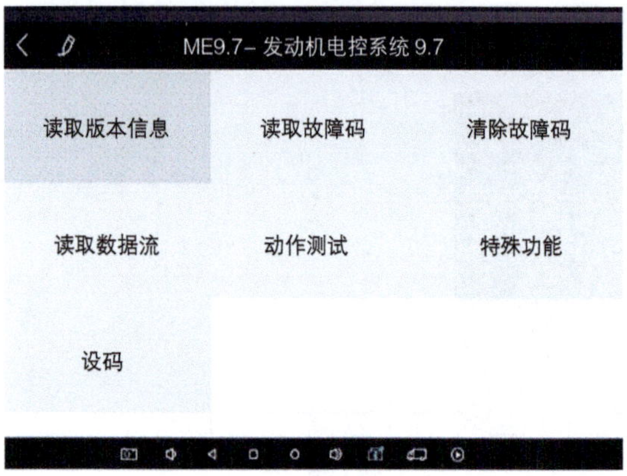

Xuǎnzé “dúqǔ shùjùliú” xuǎnxiàng.
D. 选择 “读取数据流” 选项。
Select “Data Flow Reading” option.

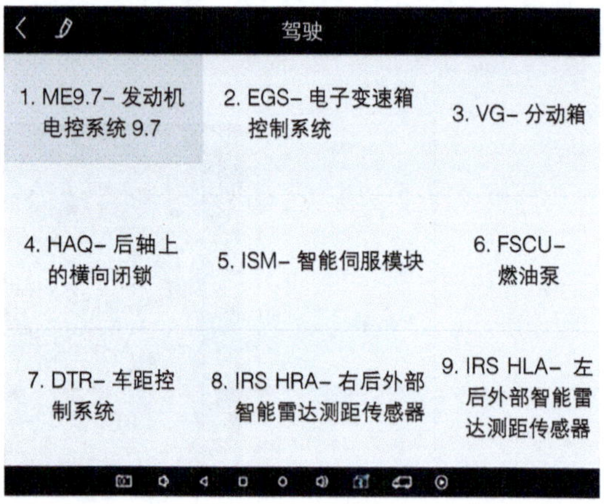

Xuǎnzé xiǎng yào cèshì de diànkòng xìtǒng.
E. 选择 想 要测试的 电控 系统。
Select the electronic control system to be tested.

2. 说一说 Let’s talk

说说故障诊断仪的操作流程。**Talk about the operation process of the fault diagnosis instrument.**

四、学以致用 xuéyǐzhìyòng Practicing What You Have Learnt

观看介绍CAN总线波形解析的相关视频，听师傅讲解波形图，将下列波形图与对应的电路情况配对。**Watch the related video introducing CAN bus waveform analysis, listen to the master’s explanation of waveform diagrams, and match the following waveform diagrams with the corresponding circuit conditions.**

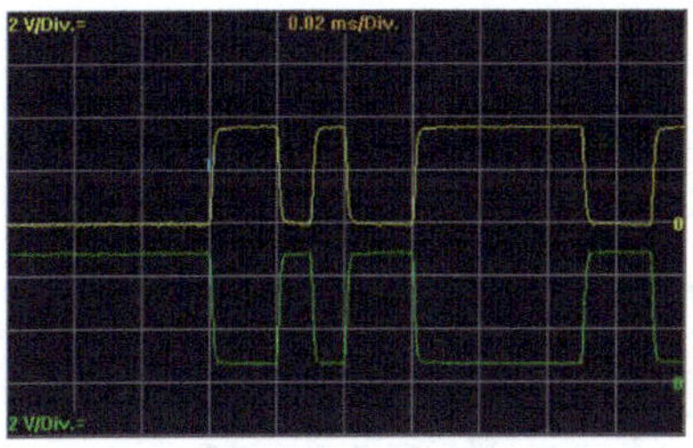

CAN-H：0.35V
CAN-L：4.65V

❶（　　）

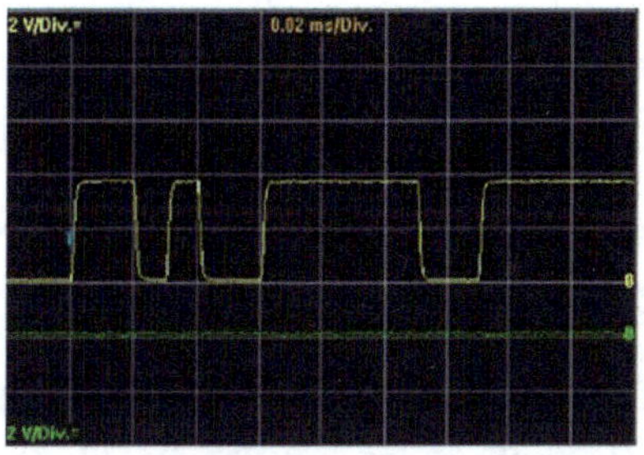

CAN-H：0.35V
CAN-L：0V

❷（　　）

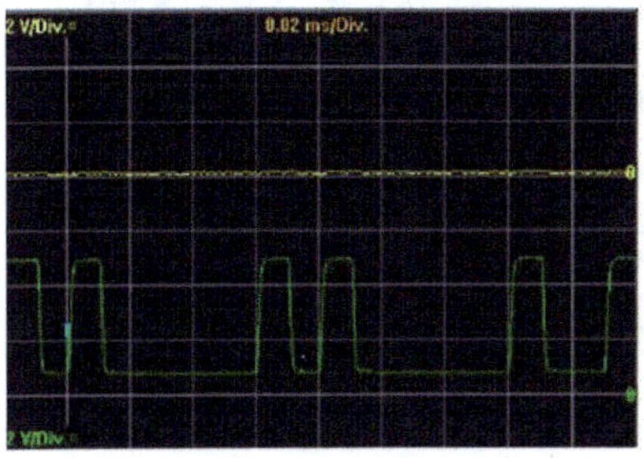

CAN-H：0V
CAN-L：4.65V

❸（　　）

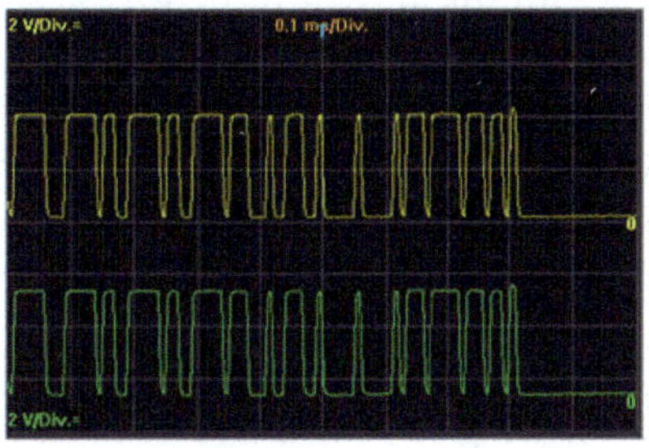

CAN-H：0.35V
CAN-L：0.35V

❹（　　）

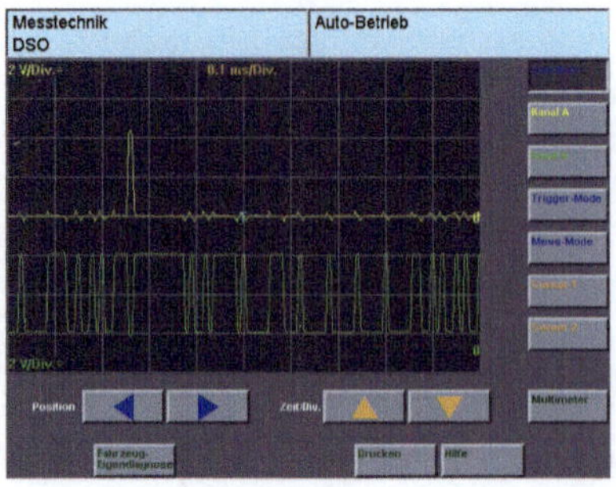

⑤（　　）

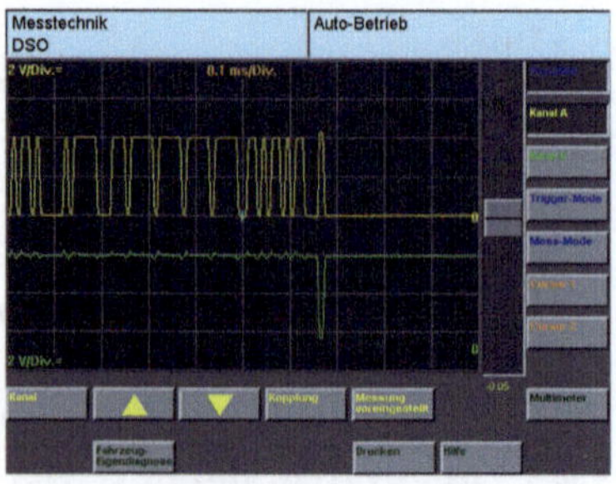

⑥（　　）

zhèngcháng
A. 正常
normal

CAN-H dātiě
D. CAN-H 搭铁
CAN-H grounding

CAN-L dātiě
B. CAN-L 搭铁
CAN-L grounding

CAN-H duànlù
E. CAN-H 断路
CAN-H open circuit

CAN-L duànlù
C. CAN-L 断路
CAN-L open circuit

CAN-L yǔ CAN-H duǎnlù
F. CAN-L 与 CAN-H 短路
CAN-L and CAN-H short circuit

五、小知识 xiǎo zhīshi Tips

Zhōngduān diànzǔ
终端 电阻

Wèile bǎozhèng CAN zǒngxiàn chuánshū shùjù de wánzhěngxìng, xiāochú zài tōngxìn diànlǎn zhōng
为了保证 CAN 总线 传输 数据的 完整性，消除 在通信 电缆 中

de xìnhào fǎnshè, zài CAN-H、 CAN-L liǎng duān gè jiāle yí gè 120 ōu de zhōngduān
的信号反射，在 CAN-H、CAN-L 两 端 各加了一个 120Ω 的 终端

diànzǔ. Gùmíng-sīyì jiù shì jiā zài zǒngxiàn mòduān de diànzǔ. Tōngguò cèliáng CAN-H、
电阻。顾名思义就是加在 总线 末端 的电阻。通过 测量 CAN-H、

CAN-L zhījiān de diànzǔzhí kěyǐ jiǎncè zǒngxiàn shìfǒu yǒu gùzhàng. Yìbān cèliáng CAN-H
CAN-L 之间的电阻值可以检测 总线 是否有 故障。一般测量 CAN-H

yǔ CAN-L zhījiān de diànzǔ wéi 60 ōu shí, dàtǐ kěyǐ pàndìng CAN zǒngxiàn shì zhèngcháng
与 CAN-L 之间的电阻为 60Ω 时，大体可以判定 CAN 总线 是 正常

de. Ruò diànzǔ wéi wúqióngdà, shuōmíng CAN zǒngxiàn duànlù; ruò diànzǔ dàyú 60 ōu,
的。若电阻为 ∞， 说明 CAN 总线 断路；若电阻大于 60Ω，

shuōmíng CAN zǒngxiàn xiànlù lǎohuà huò jiētóu yǎnghuà; ruò diànzǔ xiǎoyú 60 ōu, shuōmíng
说明 CAN 总线 线路 老化 或 接头 氧化；若电阻小于 60Ω，说明

CAN zǒngxiàn yǒu duǎnlù děng qíngkuàng fāshēng.
CAN 总线 有 短路 等 情况 发生。

Terminal Resistor

In order to ensure the integrity of the data transmitted by CAN bus and eliminate the signal reflection in the communication cable, a 120Ω terminal resistor is added to both ends of CAN-H and CAN-L. As the name implies, it is a resistor added to the bus end. By measuring the resistance value between CAN-H and CAN-L, we can detect whether the bus is faulty. Generally, when the resistance between CAN-H and CAN-L is 60Ω, it can be roughly determined that the CAN bus is normal. If the resistance is ∞, it indicates that the CAN bus is open. If the resistance is more than 60Ω, it indicates that the CAN bus is aged or the connector is oxidized. If the resistance is less than 60Ω, it indicates that there is a short circuit or other situation on the CAN bus.

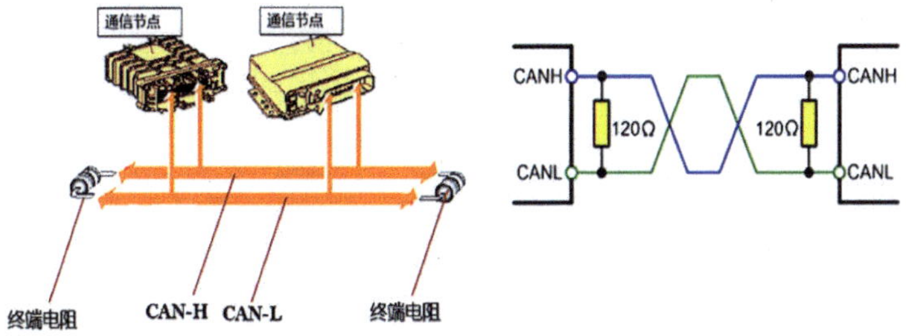

补充专业词语 bǔchōng zhuānyè cíyǔ Supplementary Specialized Vocabulary

01-07

1.	终端电阻	zhōngduān diànzǔ	phr.	terminal resistor
2.	通信电缆	tōngxìn diànlǎn	phr.	communication cable
3.	信号反射	xìnhào fǎnshè	phr.	signal reflection

第二部分 Part 2

汉字 Chinese Characters

一、汉字知识 Hànzì zhīshi Knowledge about Chinese Characters

汉字的偏旁（1） **Radicals of Chinese characters (1)**

偏旁 Radicals	例字 Examples	部件组合 Combinations	结构图示 Illustrations
口	吗	口＋马	⿰
	呢	口＋尼	⿰
	哪	口＋那	⿰
	吃	口＋乞	⿰
	啊	口＋阿	⿰
	叫	口＋丩	⿰
囗	国	囗＋玉	⿴
	图	囗＋冬	⿴

（续表）

偏旁 Radicals	例字 Examples	部件组合 Combinations	结构图示 Illustrations
女	妈	女＋马	⿰
	她	女＋也	⿰
	姓	女＋生	⿰
	娜	女＋那	⿰
亻	你	亻＋尔	⿰
	他	亻＋也	⿰
	们	亻＋门	⿰
	作	亻＋乍	⿰
	什	亻＋十	⿰
	做	亻＋故	⿰
日	时	日＋寸	⿰
	晚	日＋免	⿰
	明	日＋月	⿰
	早	日＋十	⿱
	星	日＋生	⿱

二、汉字认读与书写 Hànzì rèndú yǔ shūxiě The Recognition and Writing of Chinese Characters

认读下列词语，并试着读写构成词语的汉字。**Recognize the following words, and try to read and write the Chinese characters forming these words.**

如果　哪里　电路图　同时　传输　传感器

如	果	哪	里
电	路	图	同
时	传	输	传
感	器		

第三部分　Part 3

日常用语　*Daily Expressions*

1. 我还要再确认吗？ Wǒ hái yào zài quèrèn ma? Do I have to make a reconfirmation?
2. 我要等多久呢？ Wǒ yào děng duōjiǔ ne? How long will I have to wait?
3. 有其他的航班吗？ Yǒu qítā de hángbān ma? Do you have any other flights?

第四部分　Part 4

单元实训　*Unit Practical Training*

故障诊断仪使用

Use of a Fault Diagnosis Instrument

实训目的 Training purpose

通过实训，实训人员能够掌握故障诊断仪读取故障码和清除故障码的方法。

Through the practical training, the trainees will be able to master the method of reading fault codes and clearing fault codes using a fault diagnosis instrument.

实训步骤 Training steps

1. 教师讲解故障诊断仪的使用方法。

   The teacher explains the usage of the fault diagnosis instrument.
2. 将实训人员分成若干小组，每组 3 ～ 5 人。

   Divide the trainees into groups of 3-5.
3. 实训人员采用道通故障诊断仪读取车辆的故障码和清除故障码。

   The trainees use the AUTEL fault diagnosis instrument to read the vehicle's fault codes and clear the fault codes.

读取故障码操作：

Operation of reading fault codes:

（1）准备工位及故障诊断仪。

Prepare the workstation and fault diagnosis instrument.

（2）查看车辆信息：品牌、生产厂商、VIN 码。

Check the vehicle information, including the brand, manufacturer, VIN code.

（3）关闭点火开关。

Switch off the ignition.

（4）将蓝牙接口与车辆诊断接口（OBD-II）连接。

Connect the bluetooth interface to the vehicle diagnostic interface（OBD-II）.

（5）打开故障诊断仪开关。

Turn on the switch of the fault diagnosis instrument.

（6）打开汽车点火开关。

Switch on the ignition of the vehicle.

（7）根据检测车型选择实际操作。

Select the practical operation based on the tested vehicle model.

（8）读取故障码和清除故障码。

Read the fault codes and clear them.

（9）退出程序，关闭点火开关。

Exit the program and switch off the ignition.

（10）拔下蓝牙模块插头。

Unplug the bluetooth module plug.

4 小组间进行比赛，看哪组学员操作得规范，读取数据正确。

Conduct a competition among groups to see which group of trainees is operating properly and reading data correctly.

5 教师总结评价，实训结束。

The teacher summarizes and evaluates, and the training ends.

第五部分 Part 5

单元小结 Unit Summary

cíyǔ
词语
Vocabulary

普通词语 General Vocabulary

1.	稳	wěn	adj.	stable
2.	出	chū	v.	occur
3.	拿	ná	v.	bring
4.	每	měi	pron.	every
5.	相同	xiāngtóng	adj.	same
6.	这个	zhège	pron.	this
7.	大都	dàdū	adv.	mostly, mainly
8.	大部分	dàbùfen	n.	most, majority
9.	如果	rúguǒ	conj.	if
10.	出现	chūxiàn	v.	appear
11.	无法	wúfǎ	v.	be unable (to do sth.)
12.	读取	dúqǔ	v.	read, get
13.	信息	xìnxī	n.	information
14.	怎么	zěnme	pron.	how
15.	判断	pànduàn	v.	judge, tell

cíyǔ
词语
Vocabulary

专业词语　Specialized Vocabulary

1.	运行	yùnxíng	v.	run, operate
2.	蓝牙模块	lányá mókuài	phr.	bluetooth module
3.	接入	jiērù	v.	access
4.	第二代车载诊断系统	dì-èr dài chēzài zhěnduàn xìtǒng	phr.	on-board diagnostics II (OBD-II)
5.	接口	jiēkǒu	n.	interface
6.	国际标准	guójì biāozhǔn	phr.	international standard
7.	诊断	zhěnduàn	v.	diagnose
8.	端子	duānzǐ	n.	pin, stitch
9.	规定接口	guīdìng jiēkǒu	phr.	specified interface
10.	厂商自定义接口	chǎngshāng zìdìngyì jiēkǒu	phr.	manufacturer's custom interface
11.	采用	cǎiyòng	v.	adopt
12.	控制器局域网络	kòngzhìqì júyù wǎngluò	phr.	Controller Area Network (CAN)
13.	传输	chuánshū	v.	transmit
14.	数据	shùjù	n.	data
15.	通信	tōngxìn	v.	communicate
16.	起动	qǐdòng	v.	start
17.	波形	bōxíng	n.	waveform

补充专业词语　Supplementary Specialized Vocabulary

1.	终端电阻	zhōngduān diànzǔ	phr.	terminal resistor
2.	通信电缆	tōngxìn diànlǎn	phr.	communication cable
3.	信号反射	xìnhào fǎnshè	phr.	signal reflection

jùzi
句子
Sentences

1. 你把故障诊断仪拿过来，把蓝牙模块接入汽车第二代车载诊断系统（OBD-II）接口。
2. 诊断接口有16个端子。有几个是规定接口，其他的是厂商自定义接口。
3. 大部分车辆都是通过端子6、端子14与故障诊断仪通信，通过CAN-H、CAN-L两个CAN总线传输数据。如果CAN通信出现问题，故障诊断仪是无法读取车辆信息的，整个车辆也是无法起动的。

Chēyòng chuángǎnqì

车用传感器

Automotive Sensors

chēyòng chuángǎnqì
车用 传感器
Automotive Sensors

lúntāi yālì jiāncè xìtǒng shǐyòng de chuángǎnqì
轮胎压力监测系统使用 的传感器
Sensors Used in the Tire Pressure Monitoring System

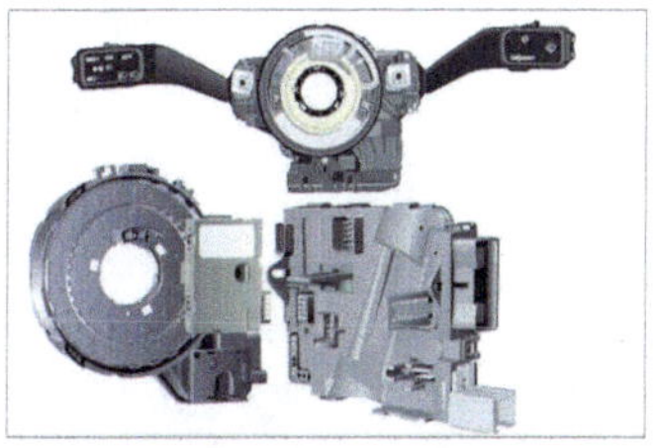

chēshēn wěndìng kòngzhì xìtǒng shǐyòng de chuángǎnqì
车身 稳定 控制 系统使用 的传感器
Sensors Used in the Vehicle Stability Control System

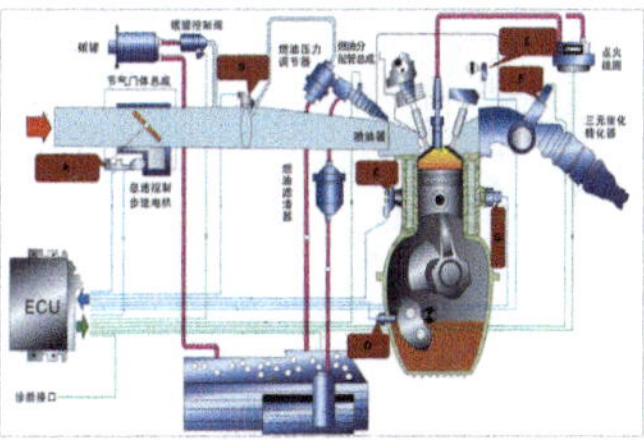

fādòngjī diànkòng xìtǒng shǐyòng de chuángǎnqì
发动机电控 系统使用 的传感器
Sensors Used in the Engine Electronic Control System

题解 Introduction

1. 学习内容：学习车用传感器的结构、功能和原理。
   Learning content: The structures, functions, and principles of automotive sensors
2. 知识目标：学习车用传感器的关键词和常用句型，学习汉字的偏旁和结构，学写相关汉字。
   Knowledge objectives: To learn the keywords and common sentence patterns for automotive sensors, learn the radicals and structures of Chinese characters, and learn to write the related Chinese characters
3. 技能目标：掌握车用传感器的匹配方法。
   Skill objective: To master the matching method of automotive sensors

第一部分 Part 1

课文 Texts

一、热身 rèshēn Warm-up

1. 给词语选择对应的图片。**Choose the corresponding pictures for the words.**

A.

B.

C.

D.

kōngqì liúliàngjì
① 空气流量计 ________
air flow meter

qūzhóu wèizhì chuángǎnqì
② 曲轴位置传感器 ________
crankshaft position sensor

yǎng chuángǎnqì
③ 氧传感器 ________
oxygen sensor

fādòngjī lěngquèyè wēndù chuángǎnqì
④ 发动机冷却液温度传感器 ________
engine coolant temperature sensor

2. 观看介绍轮胎压力监测系统的相关视频，学习汽车轮胎压力监测系统组成部件，将图中序号与对应的元件名称配对。**Watch the related video introducing tire pressure monitoring system, learn the components of automobile tire pressure monitoring system, and match the serial numbers in the picture with the corresponding component names.**

zhōngyāng xìnxī xiǎnshìqì （kě xiǎnshì lúntāi qìyā）
❶ 中央 信息显示器（可显示轮胎气压）__________________
central information display (can display tire pressure)

yòu hòu lúntāi yālì chuángǎnqì
❷ 右 后 轮胎压力 传感器 __________________
right rear tire pressure sensor

yòu qián lúntāi yālì chuángǎnqì
❸ 右 前 轮胎压力 传感器 __________________
right front tire pressure sensor

zuǒ hòu lúntāi yālì chuángǎnqì
❹ 左 后 轮胎压力 传感器 __________________
left rear tire pressure sensor

yáokòng xìnhào jiēshōuqì
⑤ 遥控 信号接收器________________
remote control signal receiver

chēshēn wěndìng kòngzhì xìtǒng （ESP）
⑥ 车身 稳定 控制 系统（ESP）________________
Electronic Stability Program (ESP)

zǔhé yíbiǎo
⑦ 组合仪表________________
combination meter

zuǒ qián lúntāi yālì chuángǎnqì
⑧ 左 前 轮胎压力 传感器 ________________
left front tire pressure sensor

二、课文 kèwén Texts

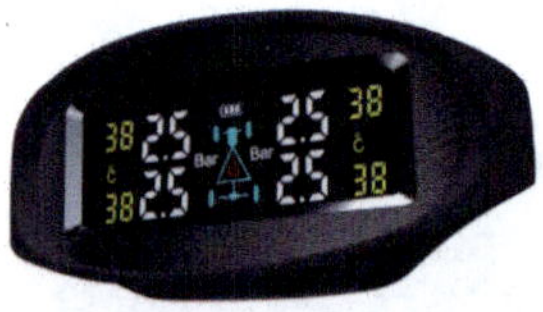

A 02-01

wéixiūgōng: Shīfu, zhè liàng chē yíbiǎo zuǒcè yǒu gè huángsè de túbiāo zài bù tíng de shǎnshuò, shì chū gùzhàng le ma?
维修工：师傅，这辆车仪表左侧有个黄色的图标在不停地闪烁，是出故障了吗？

jìshù zǒngjiān: Shì tāiyā gùzhàng zhǐshìdēng zài shǎnshuò, xiǎnshì chēliàng zuǒ hòu lúntāi de tāiyā guò dī.
技术总监：是胎压故障指示灯在闪烁，显示车辆左后轮胎的胎压过低。

wéixiūgōng: Shùzì "175" shì zhǐ zuǒ hòu lúntāi de tāiyāzhí ma?
维修工：数字“175”是指左后轮胎的胎压值吗？

jìshù zǒngjiān: Shìde, biǎoshì tāiyā 175kPa. Zhège zhí dīyú biāozhǔn yālìzhí, xūyào jiǎnchá lúntāi shìfǒu lòu qì.
技术总监：是的，表示胎压175kPa。这个值低于标准压力值，需要检查轮胎是否漏气。

wéixiūgōng: Tāiyāzhí shì tōngguò lúntāi yālì chuángǎnqì jiǎncè de ma?
维修工：胎压值是通过轮胎压力传感器检测的吗？

jìshù zǒngjiān: Shìde. Zhè liàng chē cǎiyòng de shì zhíjiēshì tāiyā jiāncè xìtǒng, lúntāi yālì
技术总监：是的。这辆车采用的是直接式胎压监测系统，轮胎压力

chuángǎnqì ānzhuāng zài chēlún nèibù, zhíjiē cèliáng tāiyā. Hái yǒu yì zhǒng
传感器安装在车轮内部，直接测量胎压。还有一种

jiànjiēshì de tāiyā jiǎncè fāngshì, yě kěyǐ jiāncè tāiyā.
间接式的胎压检测方式，也可以监测胎压。

译文 yìwén Text in English

Maintenance Technician: Master, there is a yellow icon on the left side of the dashboard of this vehicle constantly flashing. Is there a malfunction?

Technical Director: The tire pressure malfunction indicator light is flashing, indicating that the left rear tire pressure of the vehicle is too low.

Maintenance Technician: Does the number "175" refer to the left rear tire pressure value?

Technical Director: Yes, it means the tire pressure is 175kpa. It is lower than the standard pressure value. We need to check whether the tire is leaking.

Maintenance Technician: Is the tire pressure value detected by the tire pressure sensor?

Technical Director: Yes, it is. This vehicle adopts a direct tire pressure monitoring system. The tire pressure sensor is installed inside the wheel to directly measure the tire pressure. There is also an indirect tire pressure detection method, which can also monitor the tire pressure.

普通词语 pǔtōng cíyǔ General Vocabulary

02-02

1.	左侧	zuǒcè	n.	left side
2.	黄色	huángsè	n.	yellow
3.	图标	túbiāo	n.	icon
4.	不停	bù tíng	phr.	constantly
5.	显示	xiǎnshì	v.	show
6.	过低	guò dī	phr.	too low
7.	数字	shùzì	n.	number
8.	低于	dīyú	phr.	be lower than, below
9.	是否	shìfǒu	adv.	whether
10.	直接	zhíjiē	adj.	direct

专业词语 zhuānyè cíyǔ Specialized Vocabulary

02-03

1.	闪烁	shǎnshuò	v.	flash
2.	指示灯	zhǐshìdēng	n.	indicator light
3.	左后轮胎	zuǒ hòu lúntāi	phr.	left rear tire

4.	胎压值	tāiyāzhí	n.	tire pressure value
5.	标准	biāozhǔn	n.	standard
6.	压力值	yālìzhí	n.	pressure value
7.	漏气	lòu qì	phr.	leak air
8.	轮胎压力传感器	lúntāi yālì chuángǎnqì	phr.	tire pressure sensor
9.	直接式	zhíjiēshì	adj.	direct-type
10.	胎压监测系统	tāiyā jiāncè xìtǒng	phr.	tire pressure monitoring system
11.	间接式	jiànjiēshì	adj.	indirect-type
12.	监测	jiāncè	v.	monitor

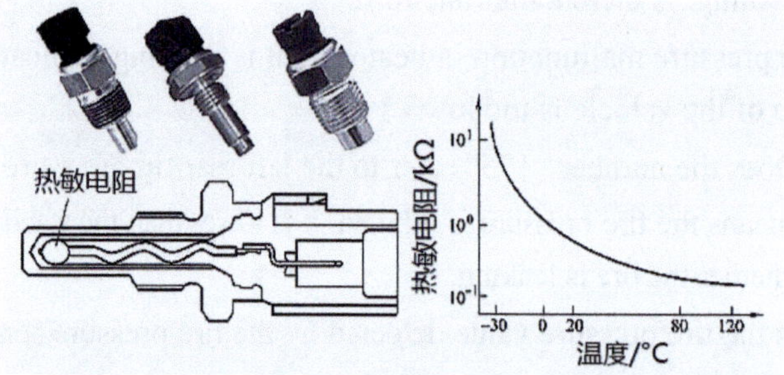

B 02-04

túdi: Shīfu, nín shǒu shang ná de zhège shì chuángǎnqì ma?
徒弟：师傅，您手上拿的这个是传感器吗？

shīfu: Shìde, zhè shì fādòngjī lěngquèyè wēndù chuángǎnqì, yìbān ānzhuāng yú fādòngjī lěngquèyèdào shang, shì yònglái jiǎncè fādòngjī lěngquèyè wēndù de. Wǒ gāng cóng chē shang chāi xialai, zhǔnbèi náqù jiǎncè. Rúguǒ jiǎncè fāxiàn lěngquèyè wēndù chuángǎnqì xìnhào yìcháng, zé yīng jìnxíng jiǎnxiū.
师傅：是的，这是发动机冷却液温度传感器，一般安装于发动机冷却液道上，是用来检测发动机冷却液温度的。我刚从车上拆下来，准备拿去检测。如果检测发现冷却液温度传感器信号异常，则应进行检修。

túdi: Qìchē shang hái yǒu biéde lèixíng de wēndù chuángǎnqì ma?
徒弟：汽车上还有别的类型的温度传感器吗？

shīfu: Qìchē shang ānzhuāngle hěn duō wēndù chuángǎnqì, lìrú jìnqì wēndù chuángǎnqì、páiqì wēndù chuángǎnqì děng, dàbùfen shì rèmǐn diànzǔshì de. Diàndòng qìchē de qūdòng diànjī yě huì yòngdào zhè zhǒng wēndù chuángǎnqì.
师傅：汽车上安装了很多温度传感器，例如进气温度传感器、排气温度传感器等，大部分是热敏电阻式的。电动汽车的驱动电机也会用到这种温度传感器。

译文 yìwén Text in English

Apprentice: Master, is this a sensor in your hand?

Master: Yes. This is an engine coolant temperature sensor, usually installed in the engine coolant pipeline to detect the engine coolant temperature. I just removed it from the vehicle and am going to test it. If the coolant temperature sensor signal is found abnormal in the test, it should be overhauled.

Apprentice: Are there other types of temperature sensors in the vehicle?

Master: There are many temperature sensors installed in the vehicle, for example, the intake air temperature sensor, exhaust air temperature sensor, etc., most of which are of thermistor-type. The drive motor of electric vehicles also uses this kind of temperature sensor.

普通词语 pǔtōng cíyǔ General Vocabulary

02-05

1.	发现	fāxiàn	v.	find
2.	则	zé	conj.	*indicating cause and effect, condition and result, etc.*
3.	应	yīng	aux.	should
4.	别的	biéde	pron.	other
5.	类型	lèixíng	n.	type
6.	例如	lìrú	v.	take for example

专业词语 zhuānyè cíyǔ Specialized Vocabulary

02-06

1.	冷却液温度传感器	lěngquèyè wēndù chuángǎnqì	phr.	coolant temperature sensor
2.	冷却液道	lěngquèyèdào	n.	coolant pipeline
3.	冷却液	lěngquèyè	n.	coolant
4.	拆	chāi	v.	disassemble
5.	异常	yìcháng	adj.	abnormal
6.	检修	jiǎnxiū	v.	overhaul
7.	进气温度传感器	jìnqì wēndù chuángǎnqì	phr.	intake air temperature sensor
8.	排气温度传感器	páiqì wēndù chuángǎnqì	phr.	exhaust air temperature sensor
9.	热敏电阻式	rèmǐn diànzǔshì	phr.	thermistor-type

三、视听说 shì-tīng-shuō Viewing, Listening and Speaking

1. 观看介绍汽车车身稳定控制系统的相关视频，学习各种传感器的特征，将图中的传感器序号与对应的名称进行配对。**Watch the related video introducing the Electronic Stability Program (ESP) of a vehicle to learn the characteristics of various sensors, and match the serial numbers of the sensors in the picture with their corresponding names.**

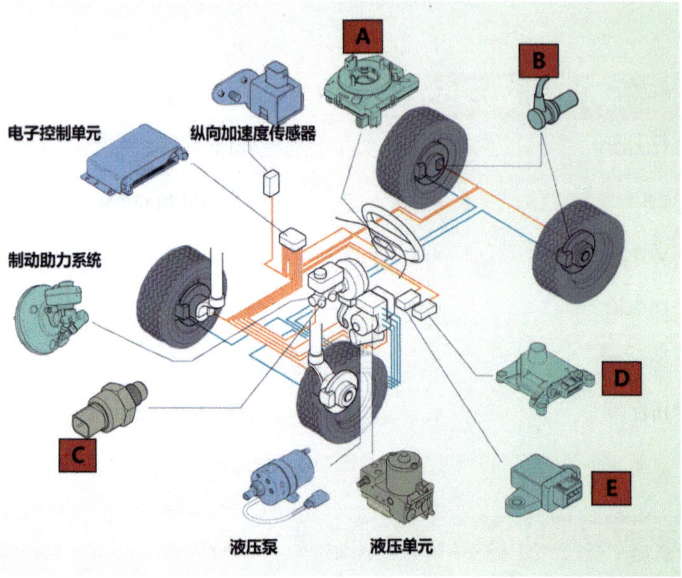

chēlún zhuànsù chuángǎnqì
❶ 车轮 转速 传感器 ________________
wheel speed sensor

héngxiàng jiāsùdù chuángǎnqì
❷ 横向 加速度 传感器 ________________
lateral acceleration sensor

fāngxiàngpán zhuǎnxiàngjiǎo chuángǎnqì
❸ 方向盘 转向角 传感器 ________________
steering angle sensor

piānzhuǎnlǜ chuángǎnqì
❹ 偏转率 传感器 ________________
deflection rate sensor

zhìdòng yālì chuángǎnqì
❺ 制动 压力 传感器 ________________
brake pressure sensor

2. 说一说 **Let's talk**

说一说各种不同传感器的特点。**Talk about the characteristics of various sensors.**

四、学以致用 xuéyǐzhìyòng Practicing What You Have Learnt

观看介绍传感器位置的相关视频，了解多种传感器的位置，将图中传感器的序号与对应的名称进行配对。**Watch the related video introducing the location of sensors, learn about the positions of various sensors, and match the serial numbers of the sensors in the picture with their corresponding names.**

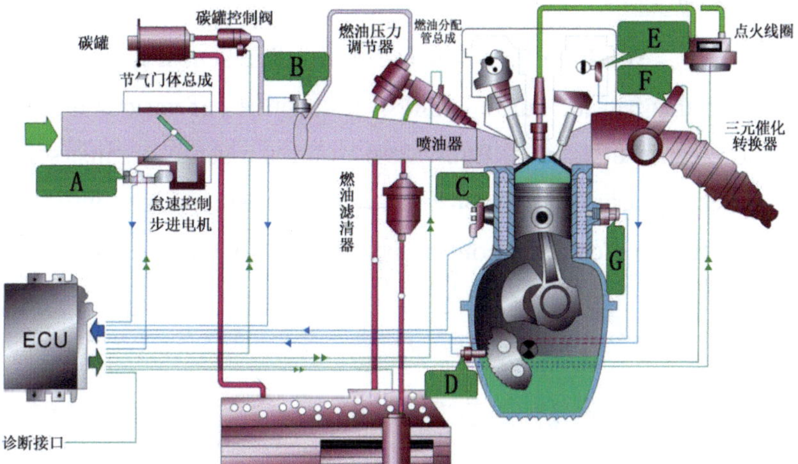

lěngquèyè wēndù chuángǎnqì
❶ 冷却液 温度 传感器 ______________
coolant temperature sensor

qūzhóu wèizhì chuángǎnqì
❷ 曲轴 位置 传感器 ______________
crankshaft position sensor

jiéqìmén wèizhì chuángǎnqì
❸ 节气门位置 传感器 ______________
throttle position sensor

yǎng chuángǎnqì
❹ 氧 传感器 ______________
oxygen sensor

jìnqì yālì wēndù chuángǎnqì
❺ 进气压力温度 传感器 ______________
intake air pressure and temperature sensor

bàozhèn chuángǎnqì
❻ 爆震 传感器 ______________
knock sensor

xiàngwèi chuángǎnqì
⑦ 相位 传感器 ______________
phase sensor

五、小知识 xiǎo zhīshi Tips

Chēyòng chuángǎnqì gōngzuò yuánlǐ
车用 传感器 工作 原理

Chuángǎnqì shì yì zhǒng néng cèliáng gèzhǒng jīxiè yùndòng zhuàngtài de wùlǐliàng, bìng
传感器是一种能测量各种机械运动状态的物理量，并

bǎ tāmen zhuǎnbiàn chéng diànliàng de zhuāngzhì. Chuángǎnqì xiāngdāng yú rén de gǎnjué qìguān,
把它们转变成电量的装置。传感器相当于人的感觉器官，

tōngguò chuángǎnqì de gǎnzhī lái zhèngquè de jiǎncè chū gèzhǒng tiáojiàn xià de wùlǐliàng. Qìchē
通过传感器的感知来正确地检测出各种条件下的物理量。汽车

chuángǎnqì shì qìchē diànzǐ kòngzhì xìtǒng de guānjiàn bùjiàn, rúguǒ méiyǒu gèzhǒng chuángǎnqì,
传感器是汽车电子控制系统的关键部件，如果没有各种传感器，

diànzǐ kòngzhì jiāng wúfǎ shíxiàn.
电子控制将无法实现。

Working Principle of Automotive Sensors

A sensor is a device that can measure the physical quantities of various mechanical motion states and convert them into electric quantities. Equivalent to human sense organs, sensors can accurately detect physical quantities in various conditions through their perception. Automotive sensors are key components of the automotive electronic control system. Without various sensors, electronic control would be impossible.

补充专业词语 bǔchōng zhuānyè cíyǔ Supplementary Specialized Vocabulary

02-07

1.	机械运动	jīxiè yùndòng	phr.	mechanical motion
2.	电量	diànliàng	n.	electric quantity
3.	电子控制	diànzǐ kòngzhì	phr.	electronic control

第二部分　Part 2

汉字　Chinese Characters

一、汉字知识　Hànzì zhīshi　Knowledge about Chinese Characters

汉字的偏旁（2）　**Radicals of Chinese characters (2)**

偏旁 Radicals	例字 Examples	部件组合 Combinations	结构图示 Illustrations
氵	汽	氵＋气	⿰
	法	氵＋去	⿰
	汉	氵＋又	⿰
	洗	氵＋先	⿰
	澡	氵＋喿	⿰
	没	氵＋殳	⿰
讠	语	讠＋吾	⿰
	课	讠＋果	⿰
	请	讠＋青	⿰
	谢	讠＋射	⿰
	词	讠＋司	⿰
	谁	讠＋隹	⿰
	认	讠＋人	⿰
	识	讠＋只	⿰
艹	节	艹＋卩	⿱
	英	艹＋央	⿱
	花	艹＋化	⿱
	苹	艹＋平	⿱
	蕉	艹＋焦	⿱

（续表）

偏旁 Radicals	例字 Examples	部件组合 Combinations	结构图示 Illustrations
辶	远	辶＋元	⿺
	这	辶＋文	⿺
	运	辶＋云	⿺
	道	辶＋首	⿺
	边	辶＋力	⿺
	选	辶＋先	⿺
	还	辶＋不	⿺

二、汉字认读与书写 Hànzì rèndú yǔ shūxiě The Recognition and Writing of Chinese Characters

认读下列词语，并试着读写构成词语的汉字。**Recognize the following words, and try to read and write the Chinese characters forming these words.**

漏气　　冷却液道　　温度传感器　　过低

漏	气	冷	却
液	道	温	度
传	感	器	过
低			

第三部分 Part 3

日常用语 *Daily Expressions*

1. 你一个人来吗？ Nǐ yí gè rén lái ma? Are you by yourself？
2. 你没有问题吧？ Nǐ méiyǒu wèntí ba? Is it all right with you?
3. 你在跟我开玩笑吧？ Nǐ zài gēn wǒ kāi wánxiào ba? Are you kidding me?

第四部分 Part 4

单元实训 Unit Practical Training

车辆胎压匹配
Vehicle Tire Pressure Matching

实训目的 Training purpose

通过实训，实训人员能够对车辆进行胎压匹配。

Through the practical training, the trainees will be able to conduct tire pressure matching for vehicles.

实训步骤 Training steps

❶ 选择 VDS2000 汽车诊断系统。

Choose VDS2000 vehicle diagnostic system.

❷ 选择"乘用车"模块，选择车型。

Select the "Passenger Car" module and select the vehicle model.

❸ 单击"开始扫描"图标，进行整车扫描。

Click the "Start Scanning" icon to perform a full vehicle scan.

❹ 找到"胎压管理"模块，单击进入胎压管理模块。

Find the "Tire Pressure Management" module, and click to enter the tire pressure management module.

❺ 单击"车辆匹配"选项卡，点击相应车轮匹配，进入胎压匹配界面。

Click the "Vehicle Matching" tab, click the corresponding wheel matching to enter the tire pressure matching interface.

❻ 拧开胎压监测模块中的气门嘴橡胶帽，对轮胎持续不间断放气，同时点击"开始匹配"图标。

Unscrew the rubber valve cap in the tire pressure monitoring module to deflate the tire continuously, and click the "Start Matching" icon at the same time.

❼ 直至系统显示"匹配成功"界面，此时该车轮已匹配成功。

The wheel has been successfully matched until the system displays the "Matching Success" interface.

❽ 重复步骤 5 ～ 7，匹配其余三个车轮。

Repeat the steps 5-7 to match the other three wheels.

❾ 教师总结评价，实训结束。

The teacher summarizes and evaluates, and the training ends.

第五部分 Part 5

单元小结 Unit Summary

cíyǔ
词语
Vocabulary

普通词语 General Vocabulary

1.	左侧	zuǒcè	n.	left side
2.	黄色	huángsè	n.	yellow

cíyǔ
词语
Vocabulary

3.	图标	túbiāo	n.	icon
4.	不停	bù tíng	phr.	constantly
5.	显示	xiǎnshì	v.	show
6.	过低	guò dī	phr.	too low
7.	数字	shùzì	n.	number
8.	低于	dīyú	phr.	be lower than, below
9.	是否	shìfǒu	adv.	whether
10.	直接	zhíjiē	adj.	direct
11.	发现	fāxiàn	v.	find
12.	则	zé	conj.	*indicating cause and effect, condition and result, etc.*
13.	应	yīng	aux.	should
14.	别的	biéde	pron.	other
15.	类型	lèixíng	n.	type
16.	例如	lìrú	v.	take for example

专业词语 Specialized Vocabulary

1.	闪烁	shǎnshuò	v.	flash
2.	指示灯	zhǐshìdēng	n.	indicator light
3.	左后轮胎	zuǒ hòu lúntāi	phr.	left rear tire
4.	胎压值	tāiyāzhí	n.	tire pressure value
5.	标准	biāozhǔn	n.	standard
6.	压力值	yālìzhí	n.	pressure value
7.	漏气	lòu qì	phr.	leak air
8.	轮胎压力传感器	lúntāi yālì chuángǎnqì	phr.	tire pressure sensor
9.	直接式	zhíjiēshì	adj.	direct-type
10.	胎压监测系统	tāiyā jiāncè xìtǒng	phr.	tire pressure monitoring system
11.	间接式	jiànjiēshì	adj.	indirect-type
12.	监测	jiāncè	v.	monitor
13.	冷却液温度传感器	lěngquèyè wēndù chuángǎnqì	phr.	coolant temperature sensor
14.	冷却液道	lěngquèyèdào	n.	coolant pipeline

cíyǔ
词语
Vocabulary

15.	冷却液	lěngquèyè	n.	coolant
16.	拆	chāi	v.	disassemble
17.	异常	yìcháng	adj.	abnormal
18.	检修	jiǎnxiū	v.	overhaul
19.	进气温度传感器	jìnqì wēndù chuángǎnqì	phr.	intake air temperature sensor
20.	排气温度传感器	páiqì wēndù chuángǎnqì	phr.	exhaust air temperature sensor
21.	热敏电阻式	rèmǐn diànzǔshì	phr.	thermistor-type

补充专业词语 Supplementary Specialized Vocabulary

1.	机械运动	jīxiè yùndòng	phr.	mechanical motion
2.	电量	diànliàng	n.	electric quantity
3.	电子控制	diànzǐ kòngzhì	phr.	electronic control

jùzi
句子
Sentences

1. 胎压故障指示灯在闪烁，显示车辆左后轮胎的胎压过低。
2. 这辆车采用的是直接式胎压监测系统，轮胎压力传感器安装在车轮内部，直接测量胎压。还有一种间接式的胎压检测方式，也可以监测胎压。
3. 汽车上安装了很多温度传感器，例如进气温度传感器、排气温度传感器等，大部分是热敏电阻式的。

3

Diànlùtú jiědú

电路图解读

Interpretation of Circuit Diagrams

Màiténg B8L qìchē diànlùtú zhōng de diànqì yuánjiàn

迈腾 B8L 汽车电路图中的电气元件

Electrical Components in the Circuit Diagram of the Magotan B8L Automobile

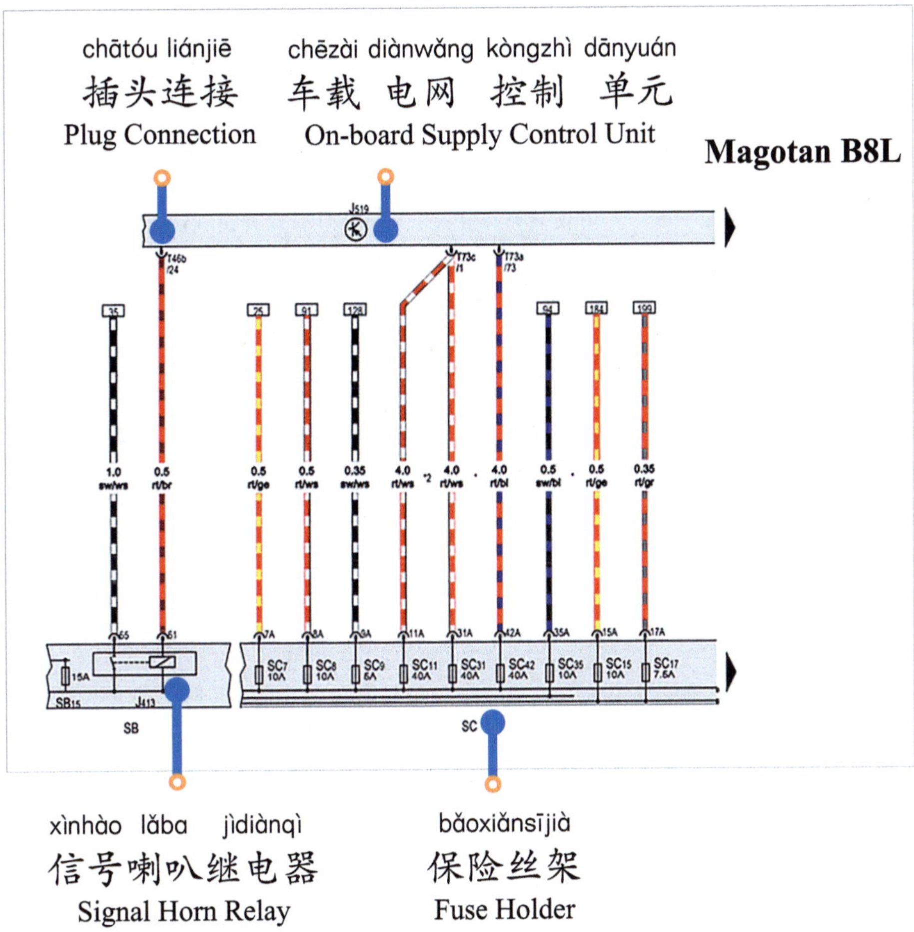

题解 Introduction

1. 学习内容：典型电路图的特点、标志、图形及文字符号的识读方法。
   Learning content: The methods of recognizing the characteristics, symbols, graphics, and textual symbols of typical circuit diagrams
2. 知识目标：学习电路图识图的关键词和常用句型，学习汉字的偏旁和结构，学写相关汉字。
   Knowledge objectives: To learn the keywords and common sentence patterns for circuit diagram recognition, learn the radicals and structures of Chinese characters, and learn to write the related Chinese characters
3. 技能目标：掌握电路图线路的查找方法。
   Skill objective: To master the method of finding circuits in a circuit diagram

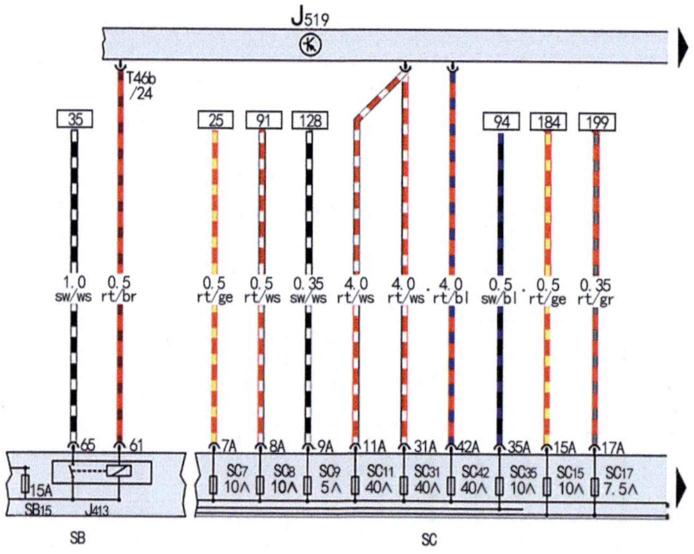

第一部分 Part 1

课文 Texts

一、热身 rèshēn Warm-up

1. 给词语选择对应的图片。**Choose the corresponding pictures for the words.**

A.

B.

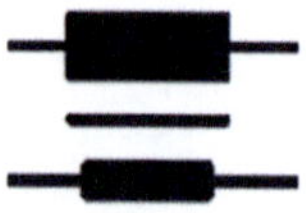

C.

D.

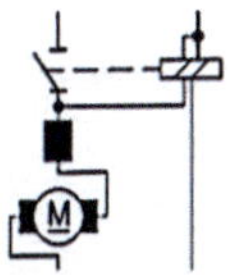
E.

F.

G.

H.

diànkòng dānyuán
❶ 电控 单元 ________________
electronic control unit

xiànquān
❷ 线圈 ________________
coil

qǐdòngjī
❸ 起动机________________
starter

jìdiànqì
❹ 继电器________________
relay

diànzǔ
❺ 电阻________________
resistance

diàncífá
❻ 电磁阀________________
solenoid valve

diǎnhuǒ xiànquān
❼ 点火 线圈 ________________
ignition coil

bǎoxiǎnsī
❽ 保险丝________________
fuse

2. 观看介绍汽车电路图电气元件的相关视频，将下面电路图中的编号代码与其所代表的元件配对。

Watch the related video introducing the electrical components of a car circuit diagram and match the numbering codes in the following circuit diagram with the components they represent.

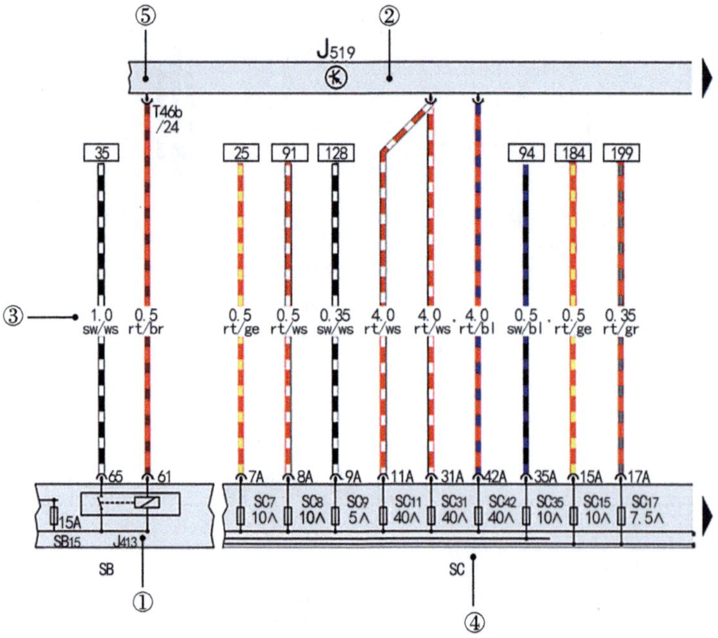

A. 保险丝架 B (bǎoxiǎnsījià)
fuse holder B

B. 信号喇叭继电器 (xìnhào lǎba jìdiànqì)
signal horn relay

C. 车载 电网 控制 单元 (chēzài diànwǎng kòngzhì dānyuán)
on-board supply control unit

D. 保险丝架 C (bǎoxiǎnsījià)
fuse holder C

E. 24 端子连接 (24 duānzǐ liánjiē)
24-pin connector

❶ J413 ________________

❷ J519 ________________

❷ SB ________________

❸ SC ________________

❺ T24b ________________

二、课文 kèwén Texts

A 03-01

túdi: Zhè liàng chē de yíbiǎopán xiǎnshì, fādòngjī gùzhàng, qǐdòngjī bú zhuàn, chēliàng
徒弟：这辆车的仪表盘显示，发动机故障，起动机不转，车辆
wúfǎ qǐdòng.
无法起动。

shīfu: Nǐ chákàn yíxiàr diànlùtú, zhǎodào qǐdòngjī de gōng diàn、dātiě hé xìnhào
师傅：你查看一下儿电路图，找到起动机的供电、搭铁和信号
kòngzhì xiànlù.
控制线路。

túdi: Ránhòu yòng wànyòngbiǎo jiǎncè xiànlù zhōng yuánjiàn de diànzǔ ma?
徒弟：然后用万用表检测线路中元件的电阻吗？

shīfu: Duì, xiān jiǎncè xiànlù zhōng de bǎoxiǎnsī hé jìdiànqì, ránhòu zài jiǎncè gè xiànlù,
师傅：对，先检测线路中的保险丝和继电器，然后再检测各线路，
kàn yíxiàr shìfǒu yǒu duànlù huò duǎnlù de qíngkuàng.
看一下儿是否有断路或短路的情况。

túdi: Wǒ mǎshàng chákàn yíxiàr diànlùtú. Búguò, lǐmiàn yǒuxiē túbiāo wǒ méi kàndǒng.
徒弟：我马上查看一下儿电路图。不过，里面有些图标我没看懂。

shīfu: Diànlùtú zhōng de zhèxiē dàimǎ fēnbié biǎoshì xìnhào lǎba jìdiànqì、chēzài diànwǎng
师傅：电路图中的这些代码分别表示信号喇叭继电器、车载电网
kòngzhì dānyuán、bǎoxiǎnsījià、bǎoxiǎnsī hé gèzhǒng xínghào de chājiēqì.
控制单元、保险丝架、保险丝和各种型号的插接器。

译文 yìwén Text in English

Apprentice: The dashboard of this vehicle shows that the engine is faulty, the starter does not work, and the vehicle cannot be started.

Master: You can check the circuit diagram and find the power supply, grounding and signal control circuits of the starter.

Apprentice: Then, should I use a multimeter to detect the resistance of the components in the circuits?

Master: Yes. First, detect the fuses and relays in the circuit, and then check each circuit to see if there is an open circuit or a short circuit.

Apprentice: I will check the circuit diagram right away. However, there are some icons I don't understand in it.

Master: These codes in the circuit diagram respectively indicate the signal horn relay, on-board supply control unit, fuse holder and fuse, and plug-in connectors of various models.

普通词语 pǔtōng cíyǔ General Vocabulary 03-02

1.	转	zhuàn	v.	rotate
2.	一下儿	yíxiàr	q.	*used after a verb to indicate one action/attempt*

3.	找到	zhǎodào	phr.	find
4.	然后	ránhòu	conj.	then
5.	对	duì	adj.	yes, right
6.	马上	mǎshàng	adv.	immediately
7.	不过	búguò	conj.	however
8.	有些	yǒuxiē	pron.	some
9.	看懂	kàndǒng	phr.	understand

专业词语 zhuānyè cíyǔ Specialized Vocabulary

03-03

1.	起动机	qǐdòngjī	n.	starter
2.	搭铁	dātiě	v.	ground
3.	信号控制线路	xìnhào kòngzhì xiànlù	phr.	signal control circuit
4.	线路	xiànlù	n.	circuit, line
5.	断路	duànlù	v.	open circuit
6.	短路	duǎnlù	v.	short circuit
7.	代码	dàimǎ	n.	code
8.	信号喇叭继电器	xìnhào lǎba jìdiànqì	phr.	signal horn relay
9.	车载电网控制单元	chēzài diànwǎng kòngzhì dānyuán	phr.	on-board supply control unit
10.	保险丝架	bǎoxiǎnsījià	n.	fuse holder
11.	插接器	chājiēqì	n.	plug connector

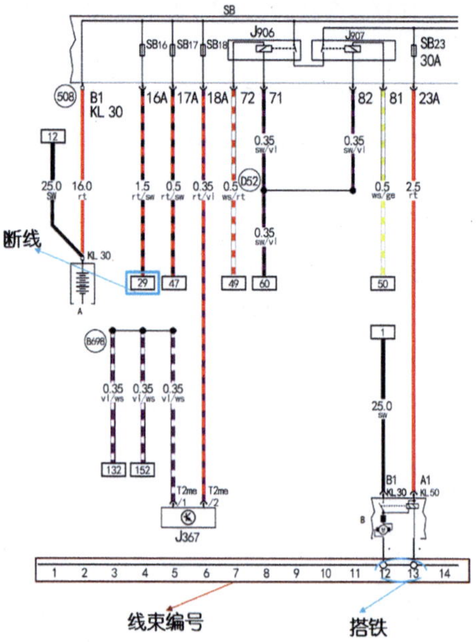

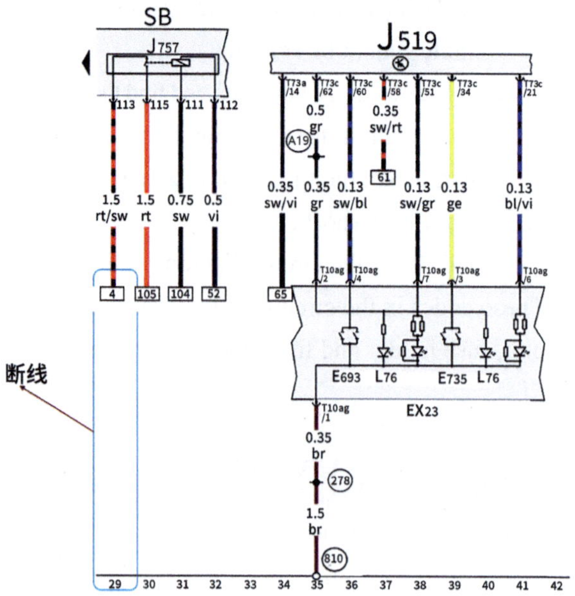

B 03-04

túdi: Shīfu, nín néngfǒu gěi wǒ jiǎng yi jiǎng diànlùtú zhōng de yìxiē cháng yòng túxíng
徒弟：师傅，您能否给我讲一讲电路图中的一些常用图形

biǎoshì de hányì?
表示的含义？

shīfu: Diànlùtú zhōng cháng yòng jiǎndān túxíng biǎoshì diànqì yuánjiàn. Xiàmiàn zhèxiē túxíng
师傅：电路图中常用简单图形表示电气元件。下面这些图形

fēnbié biǎoshì diànzǔ、xiànquān、diǎnhuǒ xiànquān、diànkòng dānyuán、qǐdòngjī、
分别表示电阻、线圈、点火线圈、电控单元、起动机、

jìdiànqì、bǎoxiǎnsī、diàncífá.
继电器、保险丝、电磁阀。

túdi: Hǎo de, wǒ jìzhù le. Lìngwài, diànlùtú zuì xiàmiàn de yì háng shùzì shì bu shì
徒弟：好的，我记住了。另外，电路图最下面的一行数字是不是

dàibiǎo dǎoxiàn liánjiē biānhào? Zài zhè zhāng tú zhōng, qǐdòngjī zài 12、13 dātiě.
代表导线连接编号？在这张图中，起动机在12、13搭铁。

shīfu: Shìde.
师傅：是的。

túdi: Nà 4 hào dǎoxiàn xiàmiàn wèi shénme biāozhù 29?
徒弟：那4号导线下面为什么标注29？

shīfu: Nà shì yīnwèi 4 hào dǎoxiàn zài cǐ yè zhōng biǎoshì bù quán, zài lìng yí yè zhōng
师傅：那是因为4号导线在此页中表示不全，在另一页中

háiyǒu liánjiē, suǒyǐ yòng duànxiàn de xíngshì biǎoshì. Xūyào qù chá lìng yí yè
还有连接，所以用断线的形式表示。需要去查另一页

zhōng de 29 hào dǎoxiàn.
中的29号导线。

译文 yìwén Text in English

Apprentice: Master, would you please tell me the meaning of some commonly used graphs in circuit diagrams?

Master: Simple graphs are often used in circuit diagrams to represent electrical components. The following graphs respectively represent the resistance, coil, ignition coil, electric control unit, starter, relay, fuse, and solenoid valve.

Apprentice: OK, I'll keep them in mind. In addition, do the numbers at the bottom of the circuit diagram represent the wire connection numbers? In this picture, the starter is grounded at 12 and 13.

Master: Yes.

Apprentice: Why is wire No.4 marked with 29 below it?

Master: That's because wire No. 4 is indicated as incomplete on this page and to be continued on another page, and it is represented in the form of a broken circuit. We need to check wire No. 29 on another page.

普通词语 pǔtōng cíyǔ General Vocabulary

03-05

1.	能否	néngfǒu	v.	*used to ask sb. politely to do sth.*
2.	给	gěi	prep.	for
3.	讲	jiǎng	v.	tell
4.	一些	yìxiē	q.	some, any
5.	常用	cháng yòng	phr.	frequently used
6.	简单	jiǎndān	adj.	simple
7.	另外	lìngwài	conj.	in addition
8.	下面	xiàmiàn	n.	below
9.	行	háng	m.	line
10.	编号	biānhào	n.	serial number
11.	标注	biāozhù	v.	mark, label
12.	因为	yīnwèi	conj.	because
13.	此	cǐ	pron.	this
14.	页	yè	n.	page
15.	全	quán	adj.	complete
16.	另	lìng	pron.	another
17.	形式	xíngshì	n.	form

专业词语 zhuānyè cíyǔ Specialized Vocabulary

03-06

1.	线圈	xiànquān	n.	coil
2.	点火线圈	diǎnhuǒ xiànquān	phr.	ignition coil
3.	电控单元	diànkòng dānyuán	phr.	electronic control unit
4.	连接	liánjiē	v.	connect
5.	断线	duànxiàn	v.	break a circuit

三、视听说 shì-tīng-shuō Viewing, Listening and Speaking

1. 观看介绍汽车电路图断线标识的相关视频，判断下列哪些线路是断线。**Watch the related video introducing the markings of broken circuits in car circuit diagrams and determine which of the following circuits are broken.**

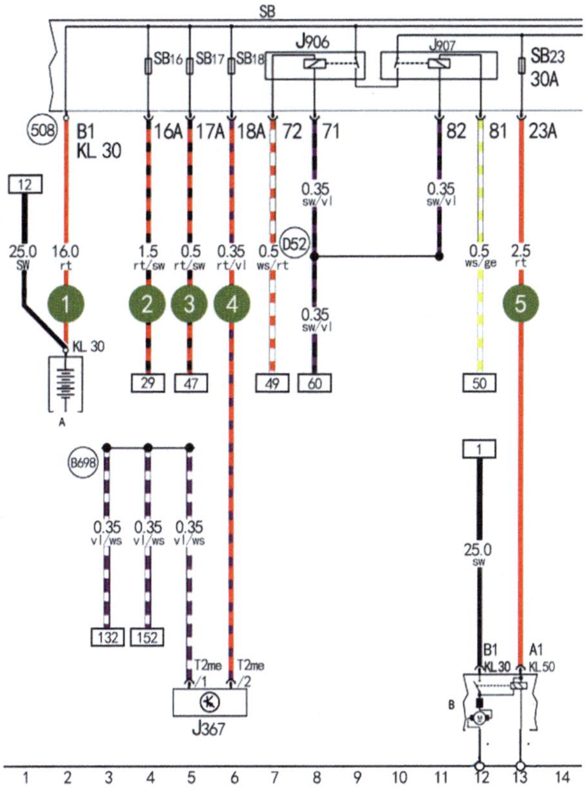

此电路图中，属于断线的线路是________。

In this circuit diagram, ________ are represented in the form of broken circuits.

2. 说一说 **Let's talk**

说一说你知道的电路图识图方法。**Talk about the circuit diagram identification methods you know.**

四、学以致用 xuéyǐzhìyòng Practicing What You Have Learnt

观看介绍汽车电路分析的相关视频，根据师傅的讲解标注下面电路图中的电流走向。**Watch the video introducing automotive circuit analysis and annotate the current direction in the circuit diagram below based on the master's explanation.**

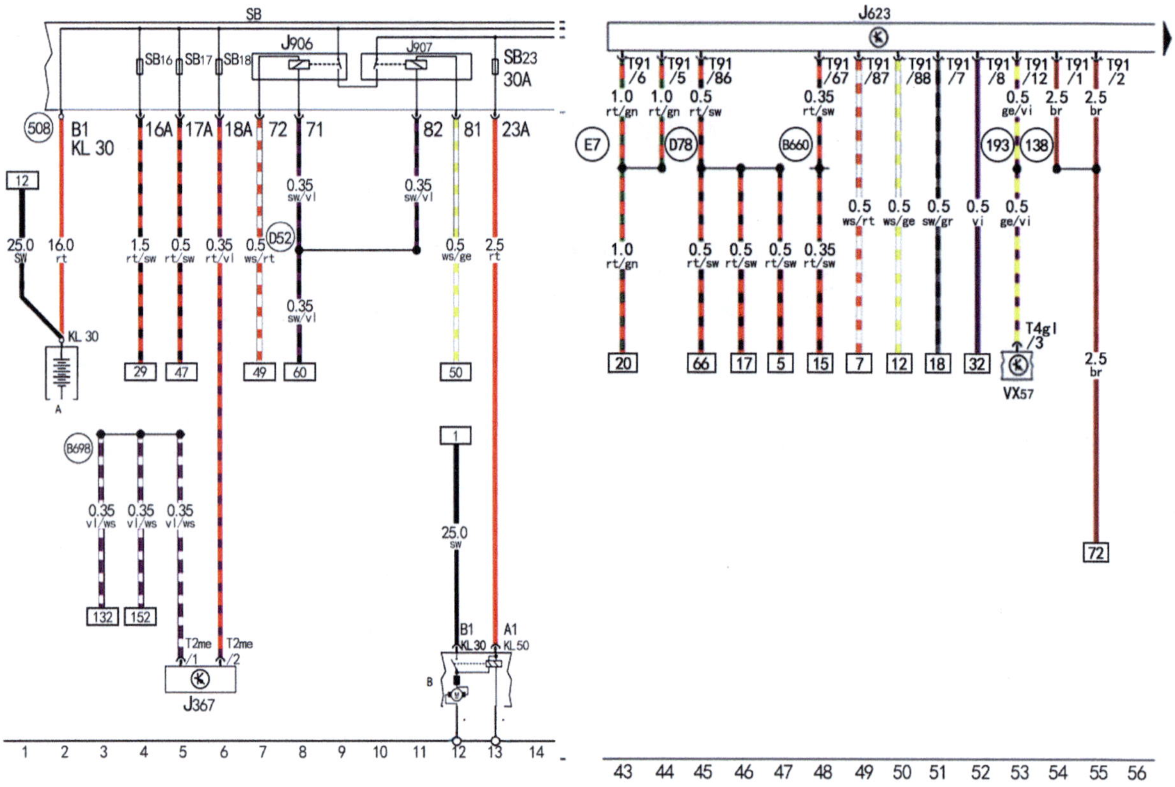

五、小知识 xiǎo zhīshi Tips

Diànlùtú biāoshí
电路图标识

Kàn xiàmiàn de diànlùtú, liǎojiě gèng duō diànlùtú biāoshí.
看下面的电路图，了解更多电路图标识。

Xiàngmù míngchēng;
1. 项目 名称;

Diànqì yuánjiàn;
2. 电气元件;

Duānzǐ dìngyì;
3. 端子定义;

Yuánjiàn;
4. 元件;

Nèibù liánjiē xiànshù míngchēng;
5. 内部连接线束 名称;

Dǎoxiàn yánsè;
6. 导线 颜色;

Dǎoxiàn biānhào;
7. 导线 编号;

T3fe-3:T3fe chātóu de dì 3 hào duānzǐ;
8. T3fe-3:T3fe 插头的第 3 号 端子;

TML: chājiēqì de míngchēng;
9. TML: 插接器 的 名称;

Duànxiàn;
10. 断线;

Nèibù liánjiē xiànshù, yuánquān nèi shùzì biǎoshì liánjiē wèizhì.
11. 内部连接线束, 圆圈 内数字表示连接位置。

Circuit Diagram Markings

Look at the circuit diagram below to learn more about circuit diagram markings.

1. Names of the items;
2. Electrical components;
3. Definition of pins;
4. Component;
5. Names of internal connecting harnesses;
6. Wire color;
7. Wire number;
8. T3fe-3: No. 3 pin of T3fe plug;
9. TML: Name of the plug-in connector;
10. Broken circuit.
11. Internal connecting harnesses, with the numbers in the circles indicating the connection positions.

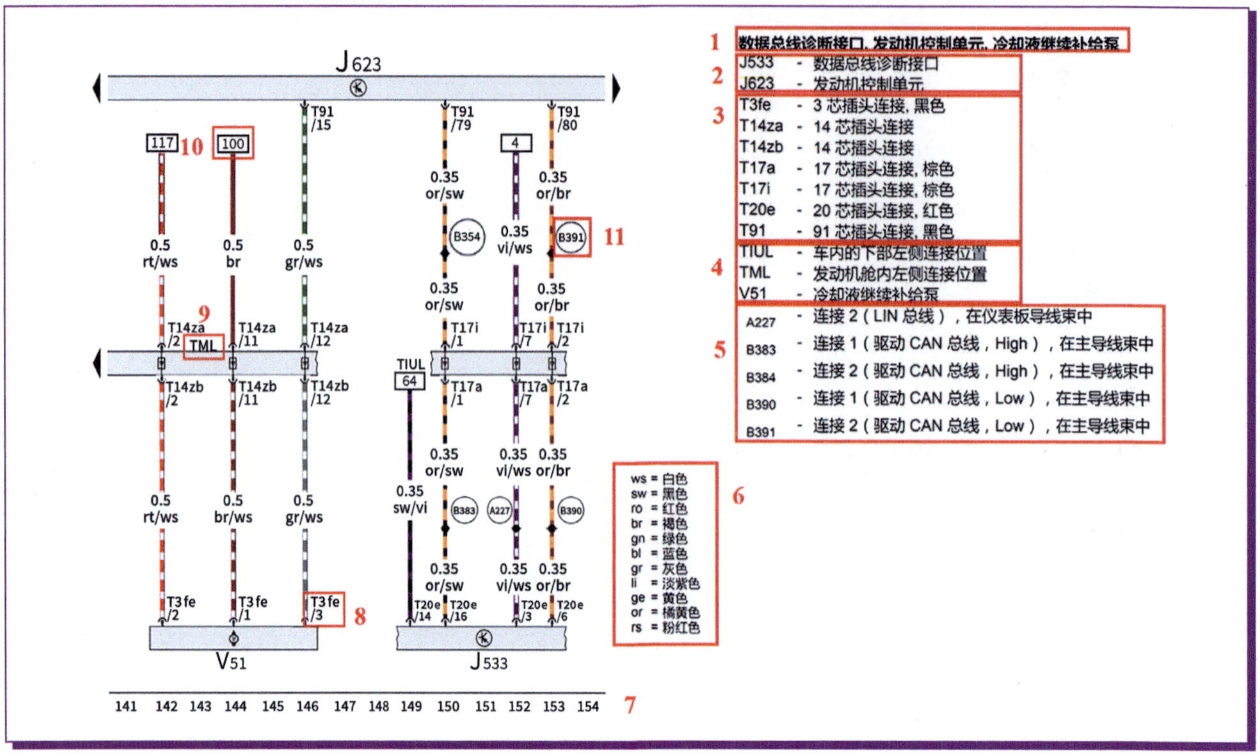

补充专业词语 bǔchōng zhuānyè cíyǔ Supplementary Specialized Vocabulary

03-07

1. 导线颜色	dǎoxiàn yánsè	phr.	wire color
2. 导线编号	dǎoxiàn biānhào	phr.	wire number

第二部分 Part 2

汉字 Chinese Characters

一、汉字知识 Hànzì zhīshi Knowledge about Chinese Characters

汉字的偏旁（3） **Radicals of Chinese characters (3)**

偏旁 Radicals	例字 Examples	部件组合 Combinations	结构图示 Illustrations
扌	打	扌＋丁	⿰
	拾	扌＋合	⿰
	报	扌＋艮	⿰
	找	扌＋戈	⿰
	排	扌＋非	⿰
	搬	扌＋般	⿰

（续表）

偏旁 Radicals	例字 Examples	部件组合 Combinations	结构图示 Illustrations
木	树	木＋对	
	机	木＋几	
	极	木＋及	
	杯	木＋不	
	校	木＋交	
	样	木＋羊	
纟	经	纟＋圣	
	红	纟＋工	
	绿	纟＋录	
	绒	纟＋戎	
心	怎	乍＋心	
	想	相＋心	
	态	太＋心	
	感	咸＋心	
	您	你＋心	
⻊	路	⻊＋各	
	跟	⻊＋艮	
	踢	⻊＋易	
	跑	⻊＋包	

二、汉字认读与书写　Hànzì rèndú yǔ shūxiě　The Recognition and Writing of Chinese Characters

认读下列词语，并试着读写构成词语的汉字。**Recognize the following words, and try to read and write the Chinese characters forming these words.**

信号　控制器　线路　保险丝架

信	号	控	制
器	线	路	保
险	丝	架	

第三部分 Part 3 日常用语 Daily Expressions

❶ 如果你们方便的话，我想现在讨论一下儿日程安排的问题。Rúguǒ nǐmen fāngbiàn dehuà,wǒ xiǎng xiànzài tǎolùn yíxiàr rìchéng ānpái de wèntí. If it's convenient for you, I would like to discuss the schedule now.

❷ 哪一天都可以？ Nǎ yì tiān dōu kěyǐ? Any day will do?

第四部分 Part 4 单元实训 Unit Practical Training

电路图线路查找方法

Method of Finding Circuits in a Circuit Diagram

实训目的 Training purpose

通过实训，实训人员能够掌握电路图线路的查找方法。

Through the practical training, the trainees will be able to master the method of finding circuits in a circuit diagram.

实训步骤 Training steps

❶ 教师布置任务，查找火花塞的供电电路图。

The teacher assigns the task to find the power supply circuit diagram of the spark plug.

❷ 将实训人员分成若干小组，每组 3 ～ 5 人。

Divide the trainees into groups of 3-5.

❸ 每组学员，查找迈腾 B8 电路图，讲述电路电流走向。

Each group of trainees searches for the circuit diagram of the Magotan B8 and describes the electric current direction of the circuit.

- 蓄电池—SB16 保险丝—J757 继电器—D206 线束——同时给 N70、N127、N291、N292 四个点火线圈供电——分别给 Q23、Q24、Q25、Q26 四个火花塞供电。

  Storage battery—SB16 fuse—J757 relay—D206 wiring harness — simultaneously supplying power to four ignition coils of N70, N127, N291 and N292 — supplying power to four spark plugs of Q23, Q24, Q25, and Q26 respectively.

- 实际控制过程中，J623 控制四个点火线圈动作，分别控制四个火花塞按次序点火。

  In the actual control process, J623 controls the action of the four ignition coils, which control the four spark plugs to ignite in sequence respectively.

❹ 每个小组比赛，看哪组学员讲述正确。

Conduct a competition among groups to see which group of trainees is speaking correctly.

❺ 教师总结评价，实训结束。

The teacher summarizes and evaluates, and the training ends.

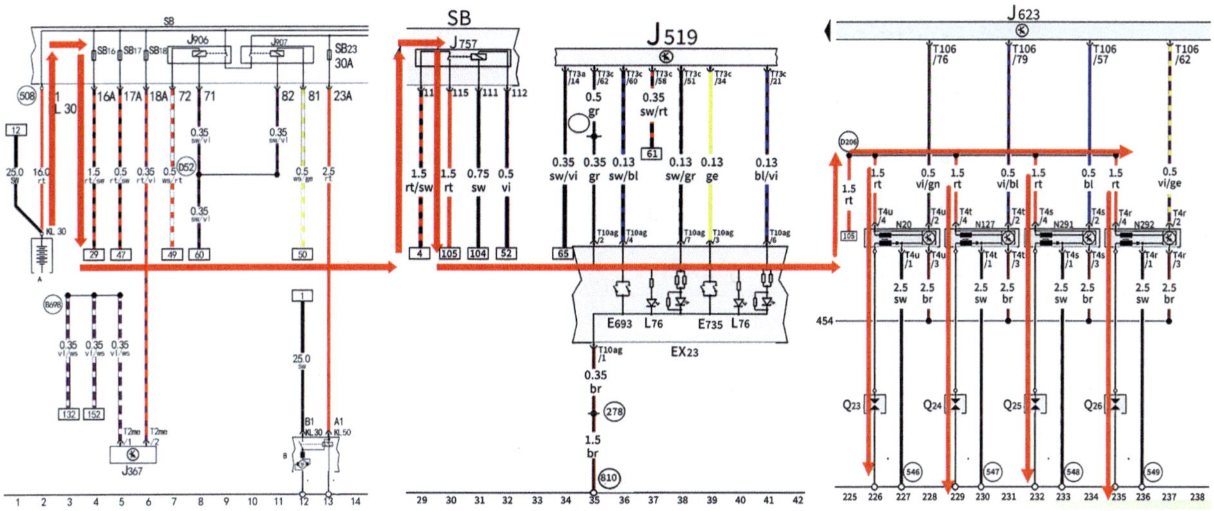

第五部分 Part 5

单元小结 Unit Summary

cíyǔ
词语
Vocabulary

普通词语 General Vocabulary

1.	转	zhuàn	v.	rotate
2.	一下儿	yíxiàr	q.	*used after a verb to indicate one action/attempt*
3.	找到	zhǎodào	phr.	find
4.	然后	ránhòu	conj.	then
5.	对	duì	adj.	yes, right
6.	马上	mǎshàng	adv.	immediately
7.	不过	búguò	conj.	however
8.	有些	yǒuxiē	pron.	some
9.	看懂	kàndǒng	phr.	understand
10.	能否	néngfǒu	v.	*used to ask sb. politely to do sth.*
11.	给	gěi	prep.	for
12.	讲	jiǎng	v.	tell
13.	一些	yìxiē	q.	some, any
14.	常用	cháng yòng	phr.	frequently used
15.	简单	jiǎndān	adj.	simple
16.	另外	lìngwài	conj.	in addition

cíyǔ
词语
Vocabulary

17.	下面	xiàmiàn	n.	below
18.	行	háng	m.	line
19.	编号	biānhào	n.	serial number
20.	标注	biāozhù	v.	mark, label
21.	因为	yīnwèi	conj.	because
22.	此	cǐ	pron.	this
23.	页	yè	n.	page
24.	全	quán	adj.	complete
25.	另	lìng	pron.	another
26.	形式	xíngshì	n.	form

专业词语　Specialized Vocabulary

1.	起动机	qǐdòngjī	n.	starter
2.	搭铁	dātiě	v.	ground
3.	信号控制线路	xìnhào kòngzhì xiànlù	phr.	signal control circuit
4.	线路	xiànlù	n.	circuit, line
5.	断路	duànlù	v.	open-circuit
6.	短路	duǎnlù	v.	short-circuit
7.	代码	dàimǎ	n.	code
8.	信号喇叭继电器	xìnhào lǎba jìdiànqì	phr.	signal horn relay
9.	车载电网控制单元	chēzài diànwǎng kòngzhì dānyuán	phr.	on-board supply control unit
10.	保险丝架	bǎoxiǎnsījià	n.	fuse holder
11.	插接器	chājiēqì	n.	plug connector
12.	线圈	xiànquān	n.	coil
13.	点火线圈	diǎnhuǒ xiànquān	phr.	ignition coil
14.	电控单元	diànkòng dānyuán	phr.	electronic control unit
15.	连接	liánjiē	v.	connect
16.	断线	duànxiàn	v.	break a ciruit

cíyǔ
词语
Vocabulary

补充专业词语　Supplementary Specialized Vocabulary

1.	导线颜色	dǎoxiàn yánsè	phr.	wire color
2.	导线编号	dǎoxiàn biānhào	phr.	wire number

jùzi
句子
Sentences

1. 先检测线路中的保险丝和继电器，然后再检测各线路，看一下儿是否有断路或短路的情况。
2. 电路图中的这些代码分别表示信号喇叭继电器、车载电网控制单元、保险丝架、保险丝和各种型号的插接器。
3. 电路图中常用简单图形表示电气元件。下面这些图形分别表示电阻、线圈、点火线圈、电控单元、起动机、继电器、保险丝、电磁阀。

4

Sān lǜ gēnghuàn

三滤更换（1）

Replacement of Three Filters (I)

jīyóu hé jīyóu lǜqīngqì de gēnghuàn bùzhòu

机油和机油滤清器的 更换 步骤

Steps of Replacing the Engine Oil and Oil Filter

nǐngsōng bìng qǔxià jīyóu lǜqīngqì

拧松 并 取下机油滤清器

Loosen and Remove the Oil Filter

bǎ jīyóu túmǒ zài O xíng mìfēngquān shang

把机油涂抹在 O 型 密封圈 上

Apply Engine Oil to the O-Ring Seal

ānzhuāng xīn de jīyóu lǜqīngqì

安装 新的机油滤清器

Install a New Oil Filter

yòng zhuānyòng bānshou nǐngjǐn lǜqīngqì

用 专用 扳手 拧紧滤清器

Tighten the Filter with a Special Wrench

题解 Introduction

1. 学习内容：机油和机油滤清器的更换步骤。
   Learning content: The steps of replacing engine oil and oil filters
2. 知识目标：学习更换机油和使用机油滤清器的关键词和常用句型，学习汉字的偏旁和结构，学写相关汉字。
   Knowledge objectives: To learn the keywords and common sentence patterns for replacing engine oil and using oil filters, learn the radicals and structures of Chinese characters, and learn to write the related Chinese characters
3. 技能目标：掌握机油、机油滤清器更换的操作方法。
   Skill objective: To master the operation methods of replacing engine oil and oil filters

第一部分 Part 1

课文 Texts

一、热身 rèshēn Warm-up

1. 给词语选择对应的图片。**Choose the corresponding pictures for the words.**

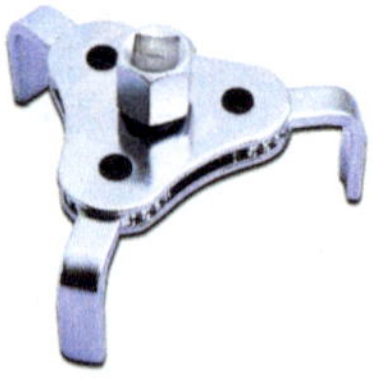

❶ ________ ❷ ________ ❸ ________ ❹ ________

jīyóu
A. 机油
engine oil

jīyóu lǜqīngqì
B. 机油滤清器
oil filter

jīyóu huíshōujī
C. 机油回收机
oil recycling machine

zhuānyòng chāi zhuāng gōngjù
D. 专用 拆 装 工具
special disassembly and assembly tools

2. 观看介绍机油功能的相关视频，选择正确的机油功能。**Watch the related video introducing engine oil functions and select the right engine oil function.**

rùnhuá
A. 润滑
lubrication

mìfēng
B. 密封
sealing

jiǎnzhèn
C. 减震
shock absorption

zhàomíng
D. 照明
lighting

lěngquè
E. 冷却
cooling

měiguān
F. 美观
beautifying

qūdòng
G. 驱动
driving

fángxiù
H. 防锈
rust prevention

jiéjìng
I. 洁净
cleaning

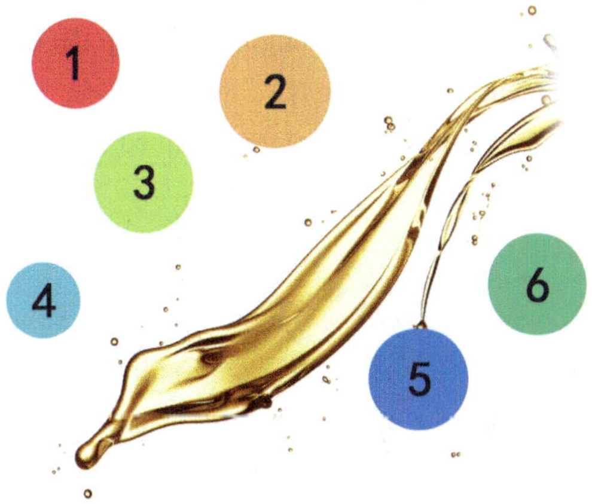

机油的六大功能包括：________________
The six major functions of engine oil include

二、课文 kèwén Texts

A 04-01

fúwù gùwèn: Nǐ hǎo, zhè liàng chē yǐjīng xíngshǐle 13000 gōnglǐ, shì bu shì xūyào zuò bǎoyǎng le? Àn bǎoyǎng shǒucè, cǐ cì bǎoyǎng xūyào gēnghuàn jīyóu、jīyóu lǜqīngqì、kōngqì lǜqīngqì、qìyóu lǜqīngqì.

服务顾问：你好，这辆车已经行驶了13000公里，是不是需要做保养了？按保养手册，此次保养需要更换机油、机油滤清器、空气滤清器、汽油滤清器。

gùkè: Jùshuō dìngqī bǎoyǎng nénggòu zuì hǎo de fāhuī chēliàng xìngnéng.

顾客：据说定期保养能够最好地发挥车辆性能。

fúwù gùwèn: Shìde, jīyóu、jīyóu lǜqīngqì xūyào tóngshí gēnghuàn. Jīyóu lǜqīngqì néng guòlǜ jīyóu zhōng dàbùfen zázhì, bǎochí jīyóu de qīngjié, yáncháng fādòngjī de shǐyòng shòumìng.

服务顾问：是的，机油、机油滤清器需要同时更换。机油滤清器能过滤机油中大部分杂质，保持机油的清洁，延长发动机的使用寿命。

gùkè: Xīnkǔ nǐ le. Chē bǎoyǎng hǎo le, qǐng tōngzhī wǒ.

顾客：辛苦你了。车保养好了，请通知我。

译文 yìwén Text in English

Service Consultant: Hello! This car has traveled 13,000 kilometers. Does it need maintenance? According to the maintenance manual, the maintenance needs to replace the engine oil, oil filter, air filter and gasoline filter this time.

Customer: It is said that regular maintenance can give full play to vehicle performance.

Service Consultant: Yes, the engine oil and oil filter need to be replaced at the same time. The oil filter can filter most of the impurities in the engine oil, keep the engine oil clean and prolong the service life of the engine.

Customer: Thank you. Please let me know after the car is maintained.

普通词语 pǔtōng cíyǔ General Vocabulary 04-02

1.	公里	gōnglǐ	m.	kilometer
2.	手册	shǒucè	n.	manual, handbook
3.	此次	cǐ cì	phr.	this time
4.	据说	jùshuō	v.	it is said
5.	能够	nénggòu	aux.	can, be able to

6.	最好	zuì hǎo	phr.	best
7.	发挥	fāhuī	v.	give play to
8.	保持	bǎochí	v.	keep
9.	延长	yáncháng	v.	prolong
10.	通知	tōngzhī	v.	notify

专业词语 zhuānyè cíyǔ Specialized Vocabulary

04-03

1.	定期保养	dìngqī bǎoyǎng	phr.	regular maintenance
2.	过滤	guòlǜ	v.	filter
3.	杂质	zázhì	n.	impurity
4.	清洁	qīngjié	adj.	clean
5.	使用寿命	shǐyòng shòumìng	phr.	service life

B

04-04

túdi: Shīfu, wǒmen xiànzài xūyào gěi zhè liàng chē fàng jīyóu ma?
徒弟：师傅，我们现在需要给这辆车放机油吗？

shīfu: Shìde, nǐ xiān yòng jīyóu huíshōujī bǎ jiù jīyóu fàng gānjìng.
师傅：是的，你先用机油回收机把旧机油放干净。

túdi: Hǎo de, wǒ yǐjīng zài sōng fàngyóu luóshuān le.
徒弟：好的，我已经在松放油螺栓了。

shīfu: Cāozuò shí yào zhùyì fángzhǐ pēnjiàn, děng shí jǐ fēnzhōng,
师傅：操作时要注意防止喷溅，等十几分钟，

jīyóu dī bu chūlái jiù biǎoshì fàng gānjìng le.
机油滴不出来就表示放干净了。

túdi: Jīyóu fàngwán hòu, zuò shénme?
徒弟：机油放完后，做什么？

shīfu: Yào bǎ fàngyóu luóshuān ànzhào guīdìng lìjǔ 30 niú mǐ zhuānghuí, wèi jiāzhù xīn de
师傅：要把放油螺栓按照规定力矩30牛·米装回，为加注新的

jīyóu zuòhǎo zhǔnbèi.
机油做好准备。

fàngyóu luóshuān
放油 螺栓
oil drain bolt

译文 yìwén Text in English

Apprentice: Master, shall we drain oil in this vehicle now?

Master: Yes. You drain the old engine oil with the oil recycling machine first.
Apprentice: OK. I'm already unscrewing the oil drain bolt.
Master: Pay attention to prevent splashing during operation. If no oil drips out after ten minutes, it's drained.
Apprentice: After the oil is drained, what shall I do next?
Master: Replace the oil drain bolt with the specified torque of 30N · m, and prepare for filling with new engine oil.

普通词语 pǔtōng cíyǔ General Vocabulary

04-05

1.	旧	jiù	adj.	old
2.	干净	gānjìng	adj.	clean
3.	松	sōng	v.	unscrew
4.	防止	fángzhǐ	v.	prevent
5.	滴	dī	v.	drip

专业词语 zhuānyè cíyǔ Specialized Vocabulary

04-06

1.	机油回收机	jīyóu huíshōujī	phr.	oil recycling machine
2.	放油螺栓	fàngyóu luóshuān	phr.	oil drain bolt
3.	操作	cāozuò	v.	operate
4.	喷溅	pēnjiàn	v.	splash
5.	规定力矩	guīdìng lìjǔ	phr.	specified torque
6.	加注	jiāzhù	v.	fill

三、视听说 shì-tīng-shuō Viewing, Listening and Speaking

1. 观看介绍机油滤清器更换相关视频，了解更换机油滤清器的步骤，并排序。**Watch the related video introducing oil filter replacement, learn about the steps of oil filter replacement, and sort them out.**

ānzhuāng xīn de jīyóu lǜqīngqì
A. 安装 新的机油滤清器
install a new oil filter

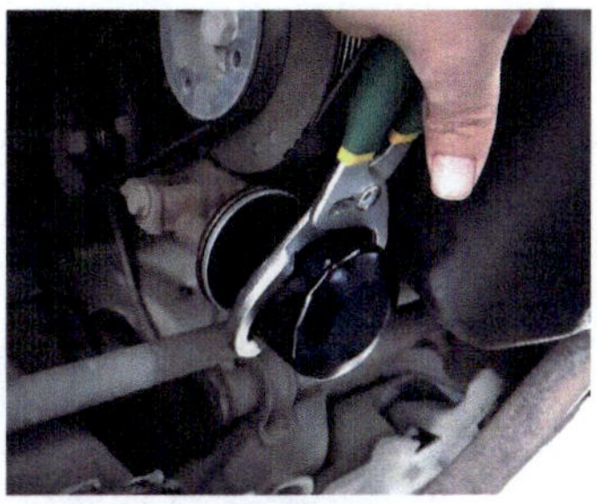

yòng zhuānyòng bānshou nǐngsōng jīyóu lǜqīngqì bìng qǔchū
B. 用 专用 扳手 拧松 机油滤清器，并 取出
use a special wrench to unscrew the oil filter and remove it

yǔ ānzhuāng biǎomiàn jiēchù hòu, yòng zhuānyòng bānshou zài nǐngjǐn 3/4 quān, nǐngjǐn lìjǔ: 15 niú mǐ
C. 与 安装 表面 接触后，用 专用 扳手 再拧紧 3/4 圈，拧紧力矩：15 牛·米
use the special wrench to tighten the filter for another 3/4 turn, with tightening torque of 15N· m after contacting with the mounting surface

bǎ fādòngjī jīyóu túmǒ zài xīn de jīyóu lǜqīngqì de O xíng mìfēngquān shang
D. 把 发动机机油涂抹在新的机油滤清器的 O 形 密封圈 上
coat the O-ring seal of the new oil filter with engine oil

2. 说一说 Let's talk

说说安装机油滤清器的步骤。 **Describe the steps for installing an oil filter.**

四、学以致用 xuéyǐzhìyòng Practicing What You Have Learnt

观看机油更换相关视频，了解机油更换的步骤，并排序。**Watch the related video about engine oil replacement, learn about the steps for engine oil replacement and sort them out.**

zhùrù xīn jīyóu
A. 注入新 机油
fill in new engine oil

xuánxià jīyóu jiāzhùkǒugài
B. 旋下机油 加注口盖
unscrew the oil filler cap

ānzhuāng fùwèi
C. 安装 复位
install and reset

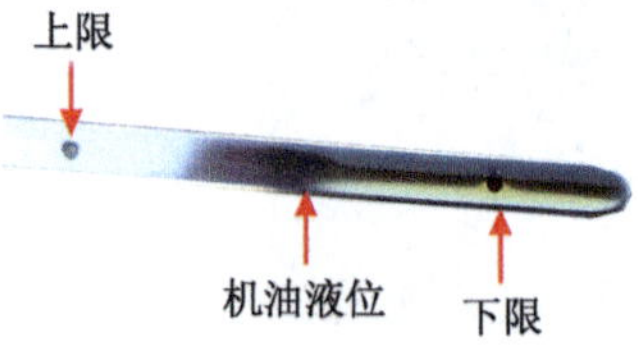

yòng jīyóu kèdùchǐ cèliáng yèwèi
D. 用 机油 刻度尺测量 液位
measure the liquid level using an oil scale

五、小知识 xiǎo zhīshi Tips

Gāo cíxìng fàngyóu luóshuān
高 磁性 放油 螺栓

Fādòngjī zài yùnxíng shí huì yǒu mósǔn, chǎnshēng jīnshǔ zázhì, luòdào yóudǐké lǐmiàn.
发动机在运行时会有磨损，产生 金属杂质，落到油底壳里面。

Rúguǒ luósī yǒu cíxìng, huì bǎ zhèxiē zázhì xīfù dào luóshuān shang. Gēnghuàn jīyóu shí,
如果螺丝有磁性，会把这些杂质吸附到 螺栓 上。更换 机油时，

kěyǐ bǎ zhèxiē zázhì pái chuqu.
可以 把这些杂质排出去。

High Magnetic Oil Drain Bolt

The engine will wear and produce metal impurities during operation, which will fall into the oil pan. If the screw has magnetism, it will adsorb these impurities onto the bolt. When replacing engine oil, these impurities can be discharged.

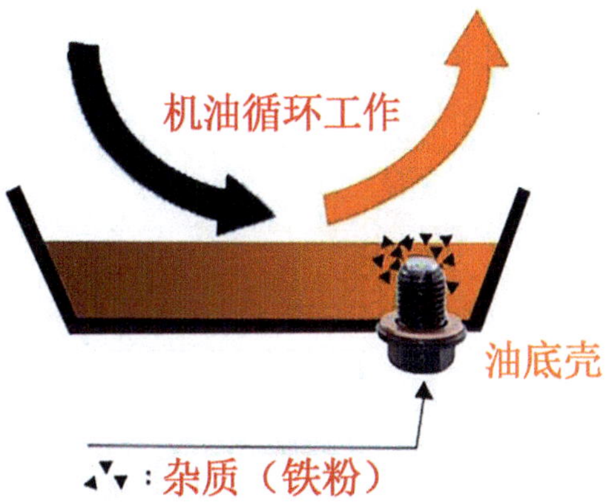

补充专业词语 bǔchōng zhuānyè cíyǔ Supplementary Specialized Vocabulary

04-07

1.	专用扳手	zhuānyòng bānshou	phr.	special wrench
2.	密封圈	mìfēngquān	n.	seal ring
3.	加注口盖	jiāzhùkǒugài	n.	filler cap
4.	刻度尺	kèdùchǐ	n.	scale
5.	磁性	cíxìng	n.	magnetism

第二部分 Part 2

汉字 Chinese Characters

一、汉字知识 Hànzì zhīshi Knowledge about Chinese Characters

汉字的偏旁（4） **Radicals of Chinese characters (4)**

偏旁 Radicals	例字 Examples	部件组合 Combinations	结构图示 Illustrations
阝(左)	阿	阝＋可	
	院	阝＋完	
	陪	阝＋音	
宀	宿	宀＋佰	
	家	宀＋豕	
	安	宀＋女	
	室	宀＋至	
	客	宀＋各	
	字	宀＋子	
	定	宀＋疋	
又	对	又＋寸	
	难	又＋隹	
	欢	又＋欠	
	友	𠂇＋又	
月	朋	月＋月	
	服	月＋𠬝	
	脑	月＋𡿺	
	期	其＋月	
钅	银	钅＋艮	
	错	钅＋昔	
	钱	钅＋戋	
	钟	钅＋中	

（续表）

偏旁 Radicals	例字 Examples	部件组合 Combinations	结构图示 Illustrations
王	玩	王＋元	⿰
	现	王＋见	⿰
	球	王＋求	⿰
	班	王＋刂＋王	⿲

二、汉字认读与书写 Hànzì rèndú yǔ shūxiě The Recognition and Writing of Chinese Characters

认读下列词语，并试着读写构成词语的汉字。**Recognize the following words, and try to read and write the Chinese characters forming these words.**

顾客　服务　定期　安装

顾				客				服				务			
定				期				安				装			

第三部分 Part 3

日常用语 *Daily Expressions*

1. 尽可能快！ Jǐn kěnéng kuài! As soon as possible!
2. 信不信由你！ Xìn bu xìn yóu nǐ! Believe it or not!
3. 下次会更好！ Xià cì huì gèng hǎo! Better luck next time!

第四部分 Part 4

单元实训 *Unit Practical Training*

机油液位检查
Engine Oil Level Checking

实训目的 Training purpose

通过本次实训，实训人员能够学会检查机油液位的方法。

Through the practical training, the trainees will be able to master the method of checking the engine oil level.

实训步骤 Training steps

1. 工具准备。
   Prepare the tools.
2. 安全防护：车辆在水平状态下静置 10 分钟以上，确保管道内机油不会回流。
   Safety protection: The vehicle is left in a horizontal state for more than 10 minutes to ensure that the engine oil in the pipeline does not flow back.
3. 取出机油刻度尺，用抹布擦拭干净。
   Take out an engine oil scale and wipe it clean with a rag.
4. 将机油刻度尺插入原位。
   Insert the engine oil scale into its original position.
5. 再次拔出刻度尺查看机油的液位。
   Take out the scale again to check the engine oil level.
6. 判断液位是否正常。
   Tell whether the liquid level is normal.
7. 车辆、工具复位。
   Reset the vehicle and tools.
8. 教师总结评价，实训结束。
   The teacher summarizes and evaluates, and ends the training.

第五部分 Part 5

单元小结 Unit Summary

cíyǔ
词语
Vocabulary

普通词语 General Vocabulary

1.	公里	gōnglǐ	m.	kilometer
2.	手册	shǒucè	n.	manual, handbook
3.	此次	cǐ cì	phr.	this time
4.	据说	jùshuō	v.	it is said
5.	能够	nénggòu	aux.	can, be able to
6.	最好	zuì hǎo	phr.	best
7.	发挥	fāhuī	v.	give play to
8.	保持	bǎochí	v.	keep
9.	延长	yáncháng	v.	prolong
10.	通知	tōngzhī	v.	notify
11.	旧	jiù	adj.	old

cíyǔ
词语
Vocabulary

12.	干净	gānjìng	adj.	clean
13.	松	sōng	v.	unscrew
14.	防止	fángzhǐ	v.	prevent
15.	滴	dī	v.	drip

专业词语 Specialized Vocabulary

1.	定期保养	dìngqī bǎoyǎng	phr.	regular maintenance
2.	过滤	guòlǜ	v.	filter
3.	杂质	zázhì	n.	impurity
4.	清洁	qīngjié	adj.	clean
5.	使用寿命	shǐyòng shòumìng	phr.	service life
6.	机油回收机	jīyóu huíshōujī	phr.	oil recycling machine
7.	放油螺栓	fàngyóu luóshuān	phr.	oil drain bolt
8.	操作	cāozuò	v.	operate
9.	喷溅	pēnjiàn	v.	splash
10.	规定力矩	guīdìng lìjǔ	phr.	specified torque
11.	加注	jiāzhù	v.	fill

补充专业词语 Supplementary Specialized Vocabulary

1.	专用扳手	zhuānyòng bānshou	phr.	special wrench
2.	密封圈	mìfēngquān	n.	seal ring
3.	加注口盖	jiāzhùkǒugài	n.	filler cap
4.	刻度尺	kèdùchǐ	n.	scale
5.	磁性	cíxìng	n.	magnetism

jùzi
句子
Sentences

1. 按保养手册，此次保养需要更换机油、机油滤清器、空气滤清器、汽油滤清器。
2. 机油滤清器能过滤机油中大部分杂质，保持机油的清洁，延长发动机的使用寿命。
3. 操作时要注意防止喷溅，等十几分钟，机油滴不出来就表示放干净了。

Sān lǜ gēnghuàn

5 三滤更换（2）Replacement of Three Filters (II)

qìyóu lǜqīngqì de gēnghuàn bùzhòu

汽油滤清器的 更换 步骤

Steps of Replacing the Gasoline Filter

zhǎodào qìyóu lǜqīngqì

找到 汽油滤清器

Find the Gasoline Filter

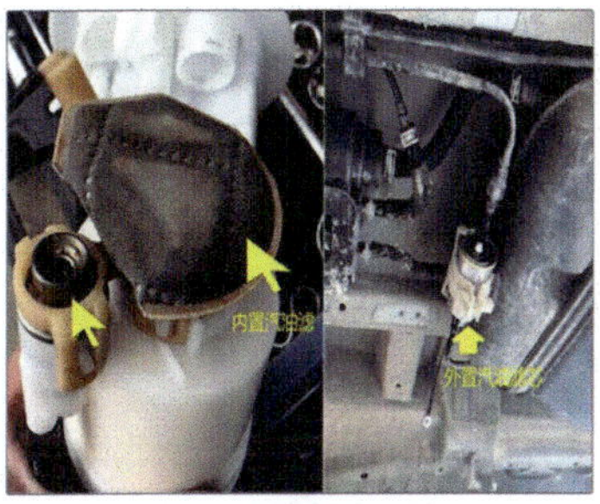

qūfēn nèizhì huò wàizhìxíng lǜqīngqì

区分内置 或 外置型 滤清器

Distinguish between the Internal and External Filters

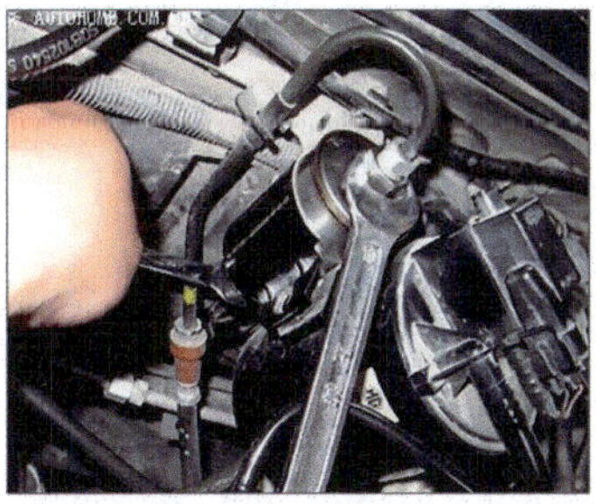

chāixià gùdìng luósī hé qiǎkòu

拆下 固定螺丝和卡扣

Remove the Fixing Screws and Buckles

ānzhuāng qìyóu lǜxīn

安装 汽油滤芯

Install the Gasoline Filter Element

kōngqì lǜqīngqì gēnghuàn bùzhòu

空气滤清器 更换 步骤

Steps of Replacing the Air Filter

dǎkāi fādòngjīcāng gài

打开发动机舱盖

Open the Engine Compartment Cover

qǔchū kōngqì lǜxīn

取出 空气 滤芯

Take out the Air Filter Element

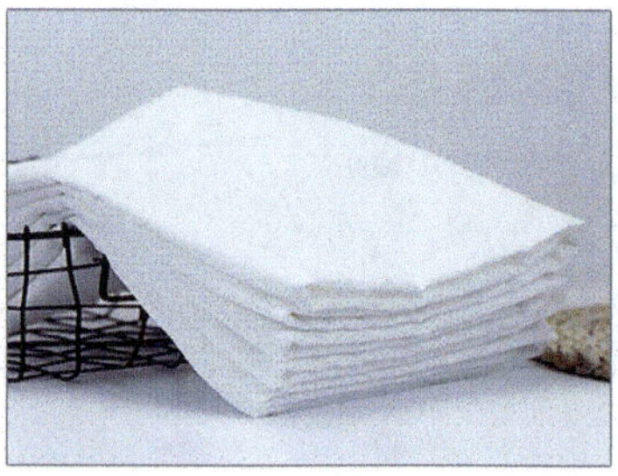

yòng gānjìng mián shābù cāshì

用 干净 棉 纱布 擦拭

Wipe with Clean Cotton Gauze

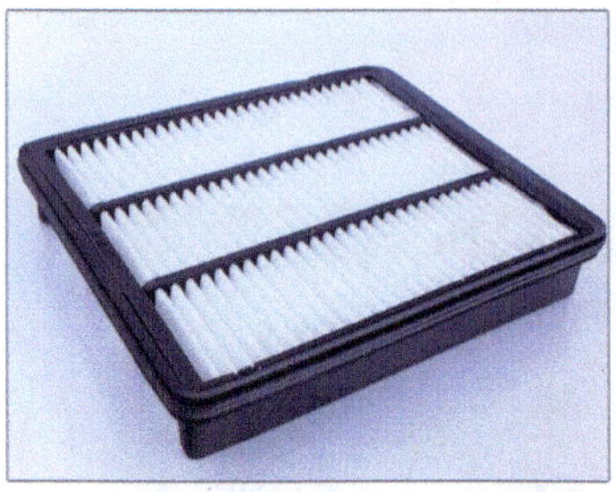

jiāngxīn de lǜxīn fàngrù lǜhé zhōng

将 新 的滤芯放入 滤盒 中

Put the New Filter Element into the Filter Cartridge

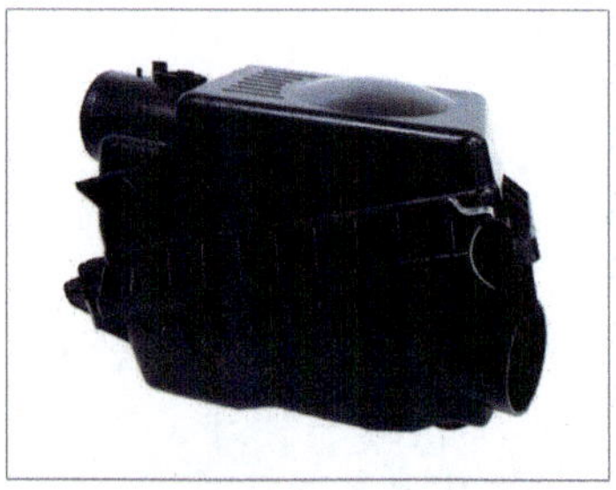

zhuānghuí kōngqì lǜqīngqì ké gàishàng fādòngjīcāng gài

装回 空气滤清器壳，盖上 发动机舱盖

Reinstall the Air Filter Housing, and Close the Engine Compartment Cover

题解 Introduction

1. 学习内容：空气滤清器和汽油滤清器的更换步骤。
   Learning content: The steps of replacing air filters and gasoline filters
2. 知识目标：学习滤清器更换的关键词和常用句型，学习汉字的偏旁和结构，学写相关汉字。
   Knowledge objectives: To learn the keywords and common sentence patterns for filter replacement, learn the radicals and structures of Chinese characters, and learn to write the related Chinese characters
3. 技能目标：掌握空气滤清器和汽油滤清器更换的操作方法。
   Skill objective: To master the operation methods of replacing air filters and gasoline filters

第一部分 Part 1

课文 Texts

一、热身 rèshēn Warm-up

1. 给词语选择对应的图片。**Choose the corresponding pictures for the words.**

① ________ ② ________ ③ ________

A. 汽油滤清器 (qìyóu lǜqīngqì) gasoline filter

B. 空气滤清器壳 (kōngqì lǜqīngqì ké) air filter housing

C. 空气滤芯 (kōngqì lǜxīn) air filter element

2. 观看介绍发动机工作原理的相关视频，了解发动机工作原理，将图中的零件与对应的词语配对。

Watch the related video introducing the working principles of the engine, learn about the working principles of the engine, and match the spare parts in the picture with the corresponding words.

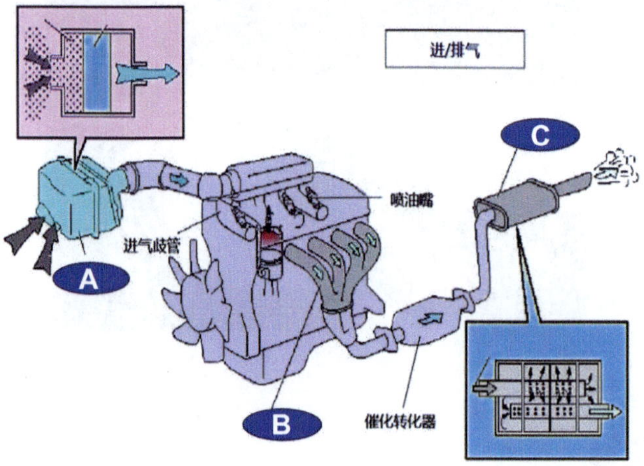

❶ 空气滤清器（kōngqì lǜqīngqì）________ air filter

❷ 消声器（xiāoshēngqì）________ muffler

❸ 排气歧管（páiqì qíguǎn）________ exhaust manifold

二、课文 kèwén Texts

A 05-01

shīfu: Zhǎochū kōngqì lǜqīngqì de wèizhì, chāixiè kōngqì lǜqīngqì. Kōngqì lǜqīngqì de wèizhì kě zài chēliàng wéixiū shǒucè zhōng cházhǎo.

师傅：找出空气滤清器的位置，拆卸空气滤清器。空气滤清器的位置可在车辆维修手册中查找。

túdì: Hǎo de, yǐjīng bǎ kōngqì lǜqīngqì ké cóng jìnqìguǎn chù qǔ xialai le, kàndào lǜxīn le.

徒弟：好的，已经把空气滤清器壳从进气管处取下来了，看到滤芯了。

shīfu: Kōngqì lǜqīngqì de lǜxīn kěyǐ lǜchú kōngqì zhōng de huīchén、shālì, bǎozhèng qìgāng
师傅：空气滤清器的滤芯可以滤除空气中的灰尘、沙粒，保证气缸

zhōng jìnrù zú liàng、qīngjié de kōngqì, qìchē bǎoyǎng shí yào dìngqī gēnghuàn. Kōngqì-
中进入足量、清洁的空气，汽车保养时要定期更换。空气

lǜxīn yìbān cǎiyòng yōuzhì lǜbù, guòlǜ miànjī dà, rónghuīliàng gāo, mìfēng
滤芯一般采用优质滤布，过滤面积大，容灰量高，密封

xìngnéng hǎo, cǎiyòng yuán chē xínghào de yuán chǎng lǜxīn xiàoguǒ gèng hǎo. Xiànzài bǎ
性能好，采用原车型号的原厂滤芯效果更好。现在把

xīn de kōngqì lǜqīngqì lǜxīn zhuāng shangqu, zhùyì zhèng-fǎnmiàn.
新的空气滤清器滤芯装上去，注意正反面。

túdì: Yǐ jiāng kōngqì lǜqīngqì lǜxīn zhuānghuíle kōngqì lǜqīngqì gài ké.
徒弟：已将空气滤清器滤芯装回了空气滤清器盖壳。

译文 yìwén Text in English

Master: Find the position of the air filter and disassemble it. The position of the air filter can be found in the vehicle maintenance manual.

Apprentice: OK. I have removed the air filter housing from the intake pipe, and I see the filter element now.

Master: The air filter element can filter out dust and sand grains in the air and ensure sufficient and clean air intake into the cylinder. Regular replacement of the air filter element is necessary during vehicle maintenance. The air filter element generally adopts high-quality filter cloth, with large filtering area, high ash capacity and reliable sealing performance. Using the original filter element of the original vehicle model results in better effect. Now install the new air filter element and pay attention to the front and back sides.

Apprentice: The air filter element has been installed back into the air filter housing.

普通词语 pǔtōng cíyǔ General Vocabulary

05-02

1.	找出	zhǎochū	phr.	find
2.	取	qǔ	v.	remove
3.	灰尘	huīchén	n.	dust
4.	沙粒	shālì	n.	sand grain
5.	足量	zú liàng	phr.	sufficient
6.	面积	miànjī	n.	area
7.	原	yuán	adj.	original
8.	效果	xiàoguǒ	n.	effect
9.	注意	zhùyì	v.	pay attention to

专业词语 zhuānyè cíyǔ Specialized Vocabulary

05-03

1.	拆卸	chāixiè	v.	disassemble
2.	壳	ké	n.	housing
3.	进气管	jìnqìguǎn	n.	intake pipe
4.	滤芯	lǜxīn	n.	filter element
5.	气缸	qìgāng	n.	cylinder
6.	更换	gēnghuàn	v.	replace
7.	优质	yōuzhì	adj.	high-quality
8.	滤布	lǜbù	n.	filter cloth
9.	容灰量	rónghuīliàng	n.	ash capacity
10.	正反面	zhèng-fǎnmiàn	n.	front and back sides

B 05-04

túdi: Shīfu, wǒmen zài jiāyóuzhàn jiā de qìyóu kàn qilai tǐng gānjìng de a, wèi shénme hái yào guòlǜ ne? Rúguǒ bú guòlǜ huì zěnyàng? Duì fādòngjī yǒu shénme yǐngxiǎng?

徒弟：师傅，我们在加油站加的汽油看起来挺干净的啊，为什么还要过滤呢？如果不过滤会怎样？对发动机有什么影响？

shīfu: Qìyóu kàn qilai hěn gānjìng, dàn qízhōng yǒu hěn duō wǒmen ròuyǎn kànbudào de fěnchén kēlì、jīxiè zázhì yǐjí jiāozhì、shuǐfèn děng.

师傅：汽油看起来很干净，但其中有很多我们肉眼看不到的粉尘颗粒、机械杂质以及胶质、水分等。

túdi: Zhème shuō lái, qìyóu lǜqīngqì de zuòyòng háishi hěn zhòngyào de!

徒弟：这么说来，汽油滤清器的作用还是很重要的！

shīfu: Shìde, rúguǒ méiyǒu jīngguò lǜqīng de qìyóu jìnrùle pēnyóuqì, qìyóu zhōng de zázhì jiù huì mósǔn huò dǔsè pēnyóuqì, shǐ pēnyóuqì bù néng zhèngcháng pēnshè rányóu. Dāng qìchē chūxiàn jiāsù huǎnmàn、jí jiāsù dùncuò děng xiànxiàng shí, kěnéng shì qìyóu lǜqīngqì lǜxīn dǔsè le.

师傅：是的，如果没有经过滤清的汽油进入了喷油器，汽油中的杂质就会磨损或堵塞喷油器，使喷油器不能正常喷射燃油。当汽车出现加速缓慢、急加速顿挫等现象时，可能是汽油滤清器滤芯堵塞了。

译文 yìwén Text in English

Apprentice: Master, the gasoline we fill at the gas station looks very clean. Why do we still have to filter it? What if we don't filter it? What is the impact on the engine?

Master: The gasoline looks clean. However, there are many dust particles, mechanical impurities, colloid and moisture that we can't see with our naked eyes.

Apprentice: So, the role of the gasoline filter is very important!

Master: Yes. If unfiltered gasoline enters the fuel injector, the impurities in the gasoline will wear or block the fuel injector, preventing the fuel injector from injecting fuel properly. When the car experiences slow acceleration, jerky acceleration, and other phenomena, may be its gasoline filter element is blocked.

普通词语 pǔtōng cíyǔ General Vocabulary

05-05

1.	看起来	kàn qilai	phr.	look
2.	挺	tǐng	adv.	quite
3.	还要	hái yào	phr.	still have to
4.	会	huì	aux.	may, can
5.	怎样	zěnyàng	pron.	how (about), what
6.	影响	yǐngxiǎng	n.	impact
7.	但	dàn	conj.	however
8.	其中	qízhōng	n.	inside
9.	肉眼	ròuyǎn	n.	naked eye
10.	经过	jīngguò	v.	go through
11.	使	shǐ	v.	cause, make
12.	现象	xiànxiàng	n.	phenomenon

专业词语 zhuānyè cíyǔ Specialized Vocabulary

05-06

1.	加油站	jiāyóuzhàn	n.	gas station
2.	粉尘	fěnchén	n.	dust
3.	颗粒	kēlì	n.	particle
4.	胶质	jiāozhì	n.	colloid
5.	水分	shuǐfèn	n.	moisture
6.	喷油器	pēnyóuqì	n.	fuel injector
7.	磨损	mósǔn	v.	wear (and tear)
8.	堵塞	dǔsè	v.	block
9.	喷射	pēnshè	v.	inject, spray
10.	缓慢	huǎnmàn	adj.	slow
11.	急加速	jí jiāsù	phr.	rapid acceleration
12.	顿挫	dùncuò	v.	stumble

三、视听说 shì-tīng-shuō Viewing, Listening and Speaking

1. 观看汽油滤清器更换相关视频，了解汽油滤清器更换的步骤，并排序。**Watch the related video about gasoline filter replacement, learn about the steps of gasoline filter replacement, and sort them out.**

chāixià gùdìng luósī hé qiǎkòu
A. 拆下固定螺丝和卡扣
remove the fixing screws and buckles

ànzhào lǜqīngqì "IN" "OUT" huòzhě "→" biāojì ānzhuāng
B. 按照滤清器"IN""OUT"或者"→"标记安装
install the filter based on the signs "IN", "OUT" or "→"

zhǎochū chēliàng qìyóu lǜqīngqì de wèizhì, qūfēn nèizhìshì hé wàizhìshì
C. 找出车辆汽油滤清器的位置，区分内置式和外置式
find the position of the vehicle's gasoline filter and distinguish between the internal type and external type

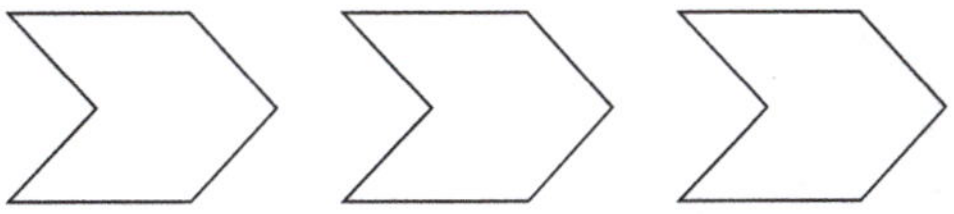

2. 说一说 Let's talk

说说更换汽油滤清器的步骤。**Describe the steps for replacing a gasoline filter.**

四、学以致用 xuéyǐzhìyòng Practicing What You Have Learnt

观看空气滤清器更换相关视频，了解空气滤清器的更换步骤，将缺少的部分补充完整。**Watch the related video about air filter replacement, learn about the steps of air filter replacement, and complete the missing parts.**

Dǎkāi cāng gài, quèrèn kōngqì lǜqīngqì ké wèizhì.
❶ 打开__1__舱盖，确认空气滤清器壳位置。
Open____compartment cover and confirm the position of the air filter housing.

Dǎkāi kōngqì lǜqīngqì ké, qǔ
❷ 打开空气滤清器壳，取__2__。
Open the air filter housing and take____ out.

Yòng cāshì kōngqì lǜqīngqì ké jí xiàtǐ nèibì.
③ 用 3 擦拭空气滤清器壳及下体内壁。
Use____ to wipe the air filter housing and the inner wall of the lower body.

Zhuānghuí gàishàng fādòngjīcāng gài.
④ 装回 4 ，盖上发动机舱盖。
Replace____, and close the engine compartment cover.

Jiāng xīn de yuán chǎng lǜxīn fàngrù lǜhé.
⑤ 将新的原厂滤芯放入滤盒。
Put the new original filter element into the filter cartridge.

kōngqì lǜxīn
A. 空气滤芯
air filter element

fādòngjī
B. 发动机
engine

kōngqì lǜqīngqì ké
C. 空气滤清器壳
air filter housing

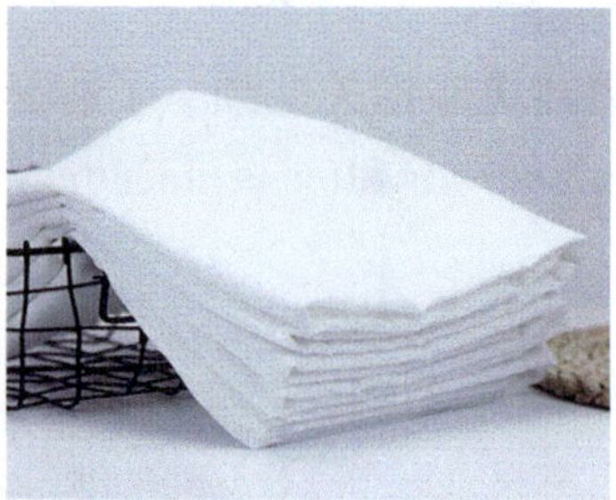

gānjìng mián shābù
D. 干净棉纱布
clean cotton gauze

五、小知识 xiǎo zhīshi Tips

Qìchē bǎoyǎng
汽车保养

Qìchē bǎoyǎng shì zhǐ dìngqī duì qìchē xiāngguān bùfen jìnxíng jiǎnchá、qīngjié、bǔjǐ、rùnhuá、tiáozhěng huò gēnghuàn mǒu xiē língjiàn de yùfángxìng gōngzuò, yòu chēng qìchē wéihù.
汽车保养是指定期对汽车相关部分进行检查、清洁、补给、润滑、调整或更换某些零件的预防性工作，又称汽车维护。

Qìchē bǎoyǎng de mùdì shì bǎochí chēliàng zhuàngkuàng zhèngcháng,
汽车保养的目的是保持车辆状况正常，

xiāochú yǐnhuàn, yùfáng gùzhàng fāshēng, yáncháng shǐyòng
消除隐患，预防故障发生，延长使用

shòumìng.
寿命。

Vehicle Maintenance

Vehicle maintenance refers to the preventive work of checking, cleaning, replenishing, lubricating, adjusting or replacing some parts of the vehicle regularly. It is also known as vehicle servicing. The purpose of vehicle maintenance is to keep the vehicle in a normal condition, eliminate hidden dangers, prevent malfunctions from occurring and prolong its service life.

补充专业词语 bǔchōng zhuānyè cíyǔ Supplementary Specialized Vocabulary

05-07

1.	固定螺丝	gùdìng luósī	phr.	fixing screw
2.	内置式	nèizhìshì	adj.	internal (type)
3.	外置式	wàizhìshì	adj.	external (type)
4.	补给	bǔjǐ	v.	supply
5.	隐患	yǐnhuàn	n.	hidden danger

第二部分 Part 2

汉字 Chinese Characters

一、汉字知识 Hànzì zhīshi Knowledge about Chinese Characters

汉字的偏旁（5） Radicals of Chinese characters (5)

偏旁 Radicals	例字 Examples	部件组合 Combinations	结构图示 Illustrations
巾	帽	巾＋冒	⿰
	帮	邦＋巾	⿱
	带	卅＋冖＋巾	⿳
广	店	广＋占	⿸
	床	广＋木	⿸
	麻	广＋林	⿸
	应	广＋⺍	⿸

（续表）

小	少	小＋丿	⿱
	尘	小＋土	⿱
	尖	小＋大	⿱
⺌	光	⺌＋兀	⿱
	当	⺌＋彐	⿱
	尝	⺌＋冖＋云	⿱
八	分	八＋刀	⿱
	公	八＋厶	⿱
	共	龷＋八	⿱
	兴	⺍＋八	⿱
	典	曲＋八	⿱
刂	到	至＋刂	⿰
	刻	亥＋刂	⿰
	别	另＋刂	⿰
	制	制＋刂	⿰

二、汉字认读与书写 Hànzì rèndú yǔ shūxiě The Recognition and Writing of Chinese Characters

认读下列词语，并试着读写构成词语的汉字。**Recognize the following words, and try to read and write the Chinese characters forming these words.**

多少　底板　分布　制冷　常用　刻度尺

多				少				底				板			
分				布				制				冷			
常				用				刻				度			
尺															

第三部分 Part 3

日常用语 Daily Expressions

1. 别太拘束！ Bié tài jūshù! Don't stand on ceremony!
2. 帮我一个忙！ Bāng wǒ yí gè máng! Give me a hand!
3. 午餐我请你。Wǔcān wǒ qǐng nǐ. I'll treat you to lunch.

第四部分 Part 4

单元实训 Unit Practical Training

更换空气滤清器
Air Filter Replacement

实训目的 Training purpose

通过本次实训，实训人员能够更换空气滤清器。

Through the practical training, the trainees will be able to replace the air filter.

实训步骤 Training steps

1. 实训场所准备车辆、工具箱，做好车辆安全防护。

   Prepare vehicles and tool boxes at the training venue, and ensure vehicle safety protection.

2. 将实训人员分成若干小组，每组 3 ～ 5 人，强调安全操作规范。

   Divide the trainees into groups of 3-5, and emphasize the safe operation practices.

3. 打开发动机舱盖，确认空气滤清器壳位置。空气滤清器的具体位置可在车辆维修手册中确定；或可根据经验确定，一般位于发动机舱左侧。

   Open the engine compartment cover and confirm the position of the air cleaner housing. The specific position of the air filter can be determined in the vehicle maintenance manual, or be determined based on experience, which is usually located on the left side of the engine compartment.

4. 打开空气滤清器壳，取出空气滤芯。注意观察是卡扣固定方式还是螺丝固定方式。

   Open the air filter housing and take out the air filter element. Pay attention to observe whether it is fixed with buckles or fixed with screws.

5. 清洁与更换。用干净棉纱布擦拭空气滤清器壳及下体内壁，将尘土清除。使用原汽车型号的新空气滤芯，将新的滤芯放入滤盒中。

   Cleaning and replacement. Wipe the air filter housing and the inner wall of the lower body with clean cotton gauze to remove the dust. Use the new air filter element of the original vehicle model and put the new filter element into the filter cartridge.

6. 与拆卸顺序相反，装回空气滤清器壳，盖上发动机舱盖。工具复位，整理工位。

   In the reverse order of disassembly, reinstall the air filter housing and put on the engine compartment cover. Reset the tools and tidy up the workstation.

⑦ 教师总结评价，实训结束。

The teacher summarizes and evaluates, and the training ends.

第五部分 Part 5

单元小结 Unit Summary

cíyǔ
词语
Vocabulary

普通词语 General Vocabulary

1.	找出	zhǎochū	phr.	find
2.	取	qǔ	v.	remove
3.	灰尘	huīchén	n.	dust
4.	沙粒	shālì	n.	sand grain
5.	足量	zú liàng	phr.	sufficient
6.	面积	miànjī	n.	area
7.	原	yuán	adj.	original
8.	效果	xiàoguǒ	n.	effect
9.	注意	zhùyì	v.	pay attention to
10.	看起来	kàn qilai	phr.	look
11.	挺	tǐng	adv.	quite
12.	还要	hái yào	phr.	still have to
13.	会	huì	aux.	may, can
14.	怎样	zěnyàng	pron.	how (about), what
15.	影响	yǐngxiǎng	n.	impact
16.	但	dàn	conj.	however
17.	其中	qízhōng	n.	inside
18.	肉眼	ròuyǎn	n.	naked eye
19.	经过	jīngguò	v.	go through
20.	使	shǐ	v.	cause, make
21.	现象	xiànxiàng	n.	phenomenon

cíyǔ
词语
Vocabulary

专业词语 Specialized Vocabulary

1.	拆卸	chāixiè	v.	disassemble
2.	壳	ké	n.	housing
3.	进气管	jìnqìguǎn	n.	intake pipe
4.	滤芯	lǜxīn	n.	filter element
5.	气缸	qìgāng	n.	cylinder
6.	更换	gēnghuàn	v.	replace
7.	优质	yōuzhì	adj.	high-quality
8.	滤布	lǜbù	n.	filter cloth
9.	容灰量	rónghuīliàng	n.	ash capacity
10.	正反面	zhèng-fǎnmiàn	n.	front and back sides
11.	加油站	jiāyóuzhàn	n.	gas station
12.	粉尘	fěnchén	n.	dust
13.	颗粒	kēlì	n.	particle
14.	胶质	jiāozhì	n.	colloid
15.	水分	shuǐfèn	n.	moisture
16.	喷油器	pēnyóuqì	n.	fuel injector
17.	磨损	mósǔn	v.	wear (and tear)
18.	堵塞	dǔsè	v.	block
19.	喷射	pēnshè	v.	inject, spray
20.	缓慢	huǎnmàn	adj.	slow
21.	急加速	jí jiāsù	phr.	rapid acceleration
22.	顿挫	dùncuò	v.	stumble

补充专业词语 Supplementary Specialized Vocabulary

1.	固定螺丝	gùdìng luósī	phr.	fixing screw
2.	内置式	nèizhìshì	adj.	internal (type)
3.	外置式	wàizhìshì	adj.	external (type)
4.	补给	bǔjǐ	v.	supply
5.	隐患	yǐnhuàn	n.	hidden danger

jùzi 句子 Sentences	1. 空气滤清器的滤芯可以滤除空气中灰尘、沙粒，保证气缸中进入足量、清洁的空气，汽车保养时要定期更换。 2. 空气滤芯一般采用优质滤布，过滤面积大，容灰量高，密封性能好，采用原车型号的原厂滤芯效果更好。 3. 如果没有经过滤清的汽油进入了喷油器，汽油中的杂质就会磨损或堵塞喷油器，使喷油器不能正常喷射燃油。当汽车出现加速缓慢、急加速顿挫等现象时，可能是汽油滤清器滤芯堵塞了。

6

Lúntāi gēnghuàn

轮胎更换

Tire Replacement

lúntāi chāixiè bùzhòu

轮胎拆卸 步骤

Steps of Disassembling Tires

jiāng chē tíng zài shuǐpíng lùmiàn

将 车 停在 水平 路面

Park the Vehicle on a Level Ground

ànzhào shùnxù nǐngsōng luóshuān

按照 顺序 拧松 螺栓

Loosen the Bolts in Order

jǔshēng chēliàng, chāixiè luóshuān, qǔxià lúntāi

举升 车辆，拆卸 螺栓，取下 轮胎

Lift the Vehicle, Dismantle the Bolts, and Remove the Tire

ānzhuāng xīn lúntāi de bùzhòu

安装 新 轮胎的步骤

Steps of Installing New Tires

jiāng lúntāi fàngzhì dào shìdàng wèizhì

将 轮胎放置 到 适当 位置

Put the Tire in the Proper Position

jiāng luóshuān xiān nǐng ruògān quān

将 螺栓 先 拧 若干 圈

Tighten the Bolts Several Turns First

àn jiāochā shùnxù jǐngù luóshuān

按交叉 顺序 紧固 螺栓

Tighten the Bolts in a Cross Order

yòng niǔlì bānshou jǐngù zhì guīdìng niǔjǔ

用 扭力扳手 紧固至 规定扭矩

Use a Torque Wrench to Tighten to the Specified Torque

fùchá

复查

Recheck

题解 Introduction

1. 学习内容：轮胎的组成、拆装辅助工具和拆装的步骤。
   Learning content: The composition of tires, auxiliary tools for disassembly and assembly, and the steps for disassembly and assembly
2. 知识目标：学习轮胎更换的关键词和常用句型，学习汉字的偏旁和结构，学写相关汉字。
   Knowledge objectives: To learn the keywords and common sentence patterns for tire replacement, learn the radicals and structures of Chinese characters, and learn to write the related Chinese characters
3. 技能目标：掌握拆装轮胎的操作方法。
   Skill objective: To master the operation method of disassembling and assembling tires

第一部分 Part 1

课文 Texts

一、热身 rèshēn Warm-up

1. 给词语选择对应的图片。**Choose the corresponding pictures for the words.**

A.

B.

C.

D.

lúntāi ❶ 轮胎________ tire	qìménzuǐ ❷ 气门嘴________ valve stem	chēlún ❸ 车轮________ wheel	luóshuān ❹ 螺栓________ bolt

2. 观看介绍轮胎拆卸的相关视频，了解轮胎拆卸步骤，然后将下列步骤排序。**Watch the related video introducing tire disassembly, learn about the steps of tire disassembly, and sort them out.**

Jǔshēng chēliàng nǐngxià luóshuān, qǔxià zuǒqiánlún.
A. 举升 车辆，拧下 螺栓，取下左前轮。
Lift the vehicle, unscrew the bolts, and remove the left front wheel.

Jiāng chē tíng zài héshì de wèizhì, chēlún bù líkāi dìmiàn.
B. 将 车 停在合适的位置，车轮不离开地面。
Park the vehicle in a proper place, with the wheels not leaving the ground.

Ànzhào jiāochā shùnxù nǐngsōng luóshuān.
C. 按照 交叉 顺序 拧松 螺栓。
Loosen the bolts in a cross order.

二、课文 kèwén Texts

A 06-01

túdi: Shīfu, jīntiān yào gēnghuàn nà tái chē de zuǒ qián chēlún.
徒弟：师傅，今天要 更换 那台车的左 前 车轮。

shīfu: Hǎo de, lāqǐ zhùchē zhìdòng, bǎ chē jǔshēng dào héshì de wèizhì, zhǔnbèi hǎo
师傅：好 的，拉起驻车制动，把车 举升 到合适的位置，准备 好

gōngjù.
工具。

túdi: Wǒ zhǔnbèile tàotǒng bānshou hé niǔlì bānshou, xiànzài kāishǐ chāi lúntāi ma?
徒弟：我准备了套筒扳手和扭力扳手，现在开始拆轮胎吗？

shīfu: Àn shùnxù nǐngxià lúntāi luóshuān.
师傅：按顺序拧下轮胎螺栓。

túdi: Hǎo de, yǐjīng bǎ zuǒ qián chēlún chāi xialai le.
徒弟：好的，已经把左前车轮拆下来了。

译文 yìwén Text in English

Apprentice: Master, I need to replace the left front wheel of the vehicle today.
Master: OK. First, pull the parking brake, lift the vehicle to a proper position, and get the tools ready.
Apprentice: I've got a socket wrench and a torque wrench. Shall I remove the tire now?
Master: Unscrew the tire bolts in sequence.
Apprentice: OK. I have already removed the left front wheel.

tàotǒng bānshou
① 套筒扳手
socket wrench

niǔlì bānshou
② 扭力扳手
torque wrench

luóshuān chāixiè shùnxù
③ 螺栓拆卸顺序
bolt disassembly sequence

普通词语 pǔtōng cíyǔ General Vocabulary

06-02

1.	拉起	lāqǐ	phr.	pull
2.	顺序	shùnxù	n.	order, sequence

专业词语 zhuānyè cíyǔ Specialized Vocabulary

06-03

1.	左前车轮	zuǒ qián chēlún	phr.	left front wheel
2.	驻车制动	zhùchē zhìdòng	phr.	parking brake
3.	套筒扳手	tàotǒng bānshou	phr.	socket wrench
4.	扭力扳手	niǔlì bānshou	phr.	torque wrench
5.	轮胎螺栓	lúntāi luóshuān	phr.	tire bolt

B 06-04

tódi: Shīfu, kāishǐ ānzhuāng xīn lúntāi ma?
徒弟：师傅，开始安装新轮胎吗？

shīfu: Xiān bǎ lúntāi gùdìng zài yuánlái de wèizhì, zài àn shùnxù jǐngù.
师傅：先把轮胎固定在原来的位置，再按顺序紧固。

túdi: Luóshuān yǐjīng jǐngù, shāowēi dǎjǐnle yìxiē.
徒弟：螺栓已经紧固，稍微打紧了一些。

shīfu: Yòng tàotǒng bānshou àn shùnxù jǐngù luóshuān. Ránhòu shǐyòng niǔlì bānshou jǐngù dào guīdìng niǔjǔ, luóshuān jǐngù hòu, yào zài jìnxíng yí cì fùchá.
师傅：用套筒扳手按顺序紧固螺栓。然后使用扭力扳手紧固到规定扭矩，螺栓紧固后，要再进行一次复查。

译文 yìwén Text in English

Apprentice: Master, shall we start installing the new tire?

Master: First, fix the tire in its original position, and then tighten it in order.

Apprentice: The bolts have been slightly tightened.

Master: Use a socket wrench to tighten the bolts in sequence. Then use a torque wrench to tighten to a specified torque, recheck after the bolts are tightened.

普通词语 pǔtōng cíyǔ General Vocabulary

06-05

1.	原来	yuánlái	adj.	original
2.	稍微	shāowēi	adv.	slightly, a little

专业词语 zhuānyè cíyǔ Specialized Vocabulary

06-06

1.	安装	ānzhuāng	v.	install
2.	固定	gùdìng	v.	fix

3.	紧固	jǐngù	v.	tighten
4.	打紧	dǎjǐn	phr.	become tight
5.	复查	fùchá	v.	recheck

三、视听说 shì-tīng-shuō Viewing, Listening and Speaking

1. 观看介绍轮胎安装的相关视频，了解轮胎安装的步骤，然后将下列步骤排序。**Watch the related video introducing tire installation, learn about the steps of tire installation, and sort them out.**

Àn shùnxù nǐngshàng luóshuān.
A. 按顺序 拧上 螺栓。
Screw the bolts in order.

Yòng tàotǒng bānshou ànzhào shùnxù jǐngù luóshuān.
B. 用 套筒 扳手 按照 顺序 紧固 螺栓。
Use the socket wrench to tighten the bolts in order.

Jiāng lúntāi gùdìng zài yuánlái de wèizhì.
C. 将 轮胎 固定 在 原来 的 位置。
Fix the tire in the original position.

Jìnxíng fùchá.
D. 进行 复查。
Recheck it.

Shǐyòng niǔlì bānshou jǐngù dào guīdìng niǔjǔ nǐngjǐn luóshuān.
E. 使用扭力扳手紧固到规定扭矩，拧紧螺栓。
Use a torque wrench to tighten the bolts to the specified torque.

2. 说一说 **Let's talk**

说说安装轮胎的步骤。**Talk about the steps to install a tire.**

四、学以致用 xuéyǐzhìyòng Practicing What You Have Learnt

观看介绍轮胎更换原因的相关视频，了解更换轮胎的原因并连线。**Watch the related video introducing the reasons for tire replacement, learn about the reasons for tire replacement, and match the columns.**

1

lúntāi dào shǐyòng niánxiàn le
A. 轮胎到使用年限了
having reached the end of a tire's durable years

②

mósǔn dào tāimiàn mósǔn biāojì
B. 磨损到胎面磨损标记
wearing to tread wear mark

③

lúntāi gǔ bāo
C. 轮胎鼓包
tire bulge

五、小知识 xiǎo zhīshi Tips

Lúntāi mósǔn biāojì
轮胎磨损标记

Tāiwén zhōngjiān yìbān dōu huì yǒu mósǔn biāojì, mósǔn biāojì de hòudù zài 2 háomǐ.
胎纹中间一般都会有磨损标记，磨损标记的厚度在 2mm。

Rúguǒ lúntāi de hòudù mósǔn zhì jùlí jíxiàn biāozhì 4 háomǐ yě jiù shì jùlí āocáo zuì shēn chù 6 háomǐ shí, jiù yīngdāng gēnghuàn lúntāi le. Xià tú hóngquān chù jiù shì mósǔn biāojì, mùcè zhè kuǎn lúntāi de mósǔn qíngkuàng yǐjīng fēicháng yánzhòng le.
如果轮胎的厚度磨损至距离极限标志 4mm（也就是距离凹槽最深处 6mm）时，就应当更换轮胎了。下图红圈处就是磨损标记，目测这款轮胎的磨损情况已经非常严重了。

Tire Wear Marks

Generally, there are wear marks in the middle of the tread pattern, and the wear marks are 2mm thick. If the tire thickness wears to 4mm away from the limit mark (i.e. 6mm away from the deepest part of the groove), the tire needs to be replaced. The wear marks are shown in the red circle in the following picture, and this tire has been seriously worn based on visual inspection.

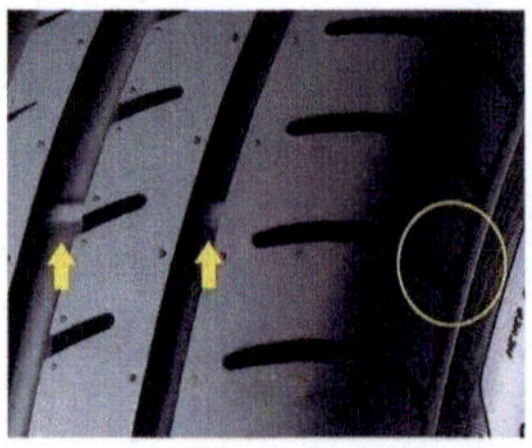

补充专业词语 bǔchōng zhuānyè cíyǔ Supplementary Specialized Vocabulary

06-07

1.	轮胎鼓包	lúntāi gǔ bāo	phr.	tire bulge
2.	使用年限	shǐyòng niánxiàn	phr.	durable years
3.	磨损标记	mósǔn biāojì	phr.	wear mark
4.	极限标志	jíxiàn biāozhì	phr.	limit mark
5.	凹槽	āocáo	n.	groove

第二部分 Part 2

汉字 Chinese Characters

一、汉字知识 Hànzì zhīshi Knowledge about Chinese Characters

汉字的偏旁（6） **Radicals of Chinese characters (6)**

偏旁 Radicals	例字 Examples	部件组合 Combinations	结构图示 Illustrations
⺮	笔	⺮＋毛	
	篮	⺮＋监	
	箱	⺮＋相	
	等	⺮＋寺	
	管	⺮＋官	
	简	⺮＋间	
	第	⺮＋弟	
灬	然	肰＋灬	
	点	占＋灬	
	热	执＋灬	
	黑	里＋灬	
	照	昭＋灬	

（续表）

偏旁 Radicals	例字 Examples	部件组合 Combinations	结构图示 Illustrations
衤	衬	衤＋寸	
	衫	衤＋彡	
	裤	衤＋库	
雨	需	雨＋而	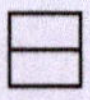
	雪	雨＋彐	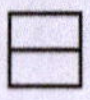
	零	雨＋令	
土	城	土＋成	
	地	土＋也	
	场	土＋𠃓	
	坏	土＋不	
	去	土＋厶	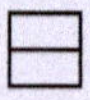

二、汉字认读与书写 Hànzì rèndú yǔ shūxiě The Recognition and Writing of Chinese Characters

认读下列词语，并试着读写构成词语的汉字。**Recognize the following words, and try to read and write the Chinese characters forming these words.**

变速箱　管理　间接式　点火　然后　零件　接地

变				速				箱				管			
理				间				接				式			
点				火				然				后			
零				件				接				地			

第三部分 Part 3

日常用语 Daily Expressions

1. 我还不能马上说定。Wǒ hái bù néng mǎshàng shuōdìng. I cannot say for certain off-hand.
2. 谢谢您的合作。Xièxie nín de hézuò. Thank you for your cooperation.
3. 如果对某些细节有意见的话，请提出来。Rúguǒ duì mǒu xiē xìjié yǒu yìjiàn dehuà, qǐng tí chulai. If you have any questions on the details, feel free to ask.

第四部分 Part 4

单元实训 Unit Practical Training

拆装轮胎总成的实训
Practical Training on Tire Disassembly and Assembly

实训目的 Training purpose

通过本次实训，实训人员能够了解轮胎拆装的步骤。

Through the practical training, the trainees will be able to learn about the steps of tire disassembly and assembly.

实训步骤 Training steps

1. 教师展示轮胎拆装的几个步骤的图片。
   The teacher shows the pictures of several steps of tire disassembly and assembly.
2. 将实训人员分成若干小组，每组 3 ~ 5 人。
   Divide the trainees into groups of 3-5.
3. 学员分组讨论轮胎拆装的步骤顺序。
   The trainees work in groups to discuss the sequence of the steps of tire disassembly and assembly.
4. 抽取一个小组，展示小组结论，并给出轮胎拆装的步骤顺序。
   Select a group to demonstrate their conclusions and provide the sequence of the steps of tire disassembly and assembly.
5. 教师总结评价，实训结束。
   The teacher summarizes and evaluates, and the training ends.

第五部分 Part 5

单元小结 Unit Summary

cíyǔ 词语 Vocabulary

普通词语 General Vocabulary

1.	拉起	lāqǐ	phr.	pull
2.	顺序	shùnxù	n.	order, sequence
3.	原来	yuánlái	adj.	original
4.	稍微	shāowēi	adv.	slightly, a little

专业词语 Specialized Vocabulary

1.	左前车轮	zuǒ qián chēlún	phr.	left front wheel
2.	驻车制动	zhùchē zhìdòng	phr.	parking brake
3.	套筒扳手	tàotǒng bānshou	phr.	socket wrench
4.	扭力扳手	niǔlì bānshou	phr.	torque wrench
5.	轮胎螺栓	lúntāi luóshuān	phr.	tire bolt
6.	安装	ānzhuāng	v.	install
7.	固定	gùdìng	v.	fix
8.	紧固	jǐngù	v.	tighten
9.	打紧	dǎjǐn	phr.	become tighten
10.	复查	fùchá	v.	recheck

补充专业词语 Supplementary Specialized Vocabulary

1.	使用年限	shǐyòng niánxiàn	phr.	durable years
2.	磨损标记	mósǔn biāojì	phr.	wear mark
3.	轮胎鼓包	lúntāi gǔ bāo	phr.	tire bulge
4.	极限标志	jíxiàn biāozhì	phr.	limit mark
5.	凹槽	āocáo	n.	groove

jùzi 句子 Sentences

1. 轮胎拆卸步骤：将车停在合适的位置，车轮不离开地面；按照交叉顺序拧松螺栓；举升车辆，拧下螺栓，取下左前轮。
2. 轮胎安装步骤：将轮胎固定在原来的位置；按顺序拧上螺栓；用套筒扳手按照顺序紧固螺栓；使用扭力扳手紧固到规定扭矩，拧紧螺栓；进行复查。
3. 轮胎更换条件：轮胎磨损到胎面磨损标记；轮胎鼓包；轮胎到使用年限了。

7

Fādòngjī diànkòng xìtǒng jiǎncè

发动机电控系统检测

Engine Electronic Control System Detection

fādòngjī diànkòng xìtǒng

发动机电控 系统

zhǔyào gùzhàng

主要 故障

Main Faults of the Engine Electronic Control System

jìdiànqì gùzhàng

继电器故障

Relay Fault

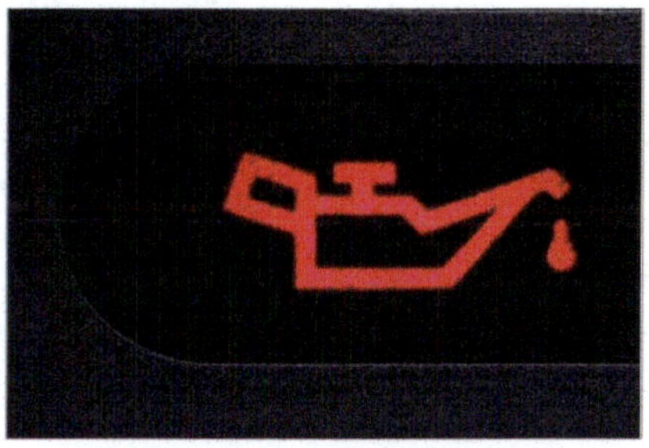

jīyóu yālì gùzhàng

机油压力故障

Engine Oil Pressure Fault

fādòngjī zhuànsù wéi líng gùzhàng

发动机 转速 为 零 故障

Zero Engine Speed Fault

题解 Introduction

1. 学习内容：发动机电控系统的常规检测，包括继电器故障、机油压力故障等。
   Learning content: The routine detection of engine electronic control system, including relay faults, engine oil pressure faults, etc.
2. 知识目标：学习发动机电控系统常规检测的关键词和常用句型，学习汉字的偏旁和结构，学写相关汉字。
   Knowledge objectives: To learn the keywords and common sentence patterns for routine detection of engine electronic control system, learn the radicals and structures of Chinese characters, and learn to write the related Chinese characters
3. 技能目标：掌握发动机电控系统常规检测的操作方法。
   Skill objective: To master the operation method of routine detection of engine electronic control system

第一部分 Part 1

课文 *Texts*

一、热身 rèshēn Warm-up

1. 给词语选择对应的图片。**Choose the corresponding pictures for the words.**

A.

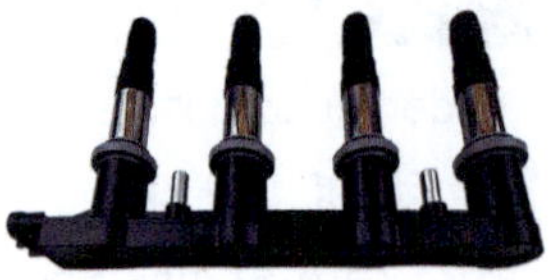

B.

C.

D.

jìdiànqì
❶ 继电器________
relay

gùzhàng zhěnduànyí
❷ 故障 诊断仪________
fault diagnosis instrument

jīyóu yālì bàojǐngdēng
❸ 机油压力 报警灯________
engine oil pressure alarm lamp

diǎnhuǒ xiànquān
❹ 点火 线圈________
ignition coil

2. 观看介绍发动机电控系统组成相关视频，选出发动机电控系统的控制内容。**Watch the related video introducing the components of the engine electronic control system and select the content controlled by the engine electronic control system.**

diànkòng diǎnhuǒ xìtǒng
A. 电控 点火 系统
electronic ignition system

zēngyā kòngzhì xìtǒng
B. 增压 控制 系统
supercharging control system

shīxiào bǎohù xìtǒng
C. 失效保护系统
fail-safe system

zìzhěnduàn yǔ bàojǐng xìtǒng
D. 自诊断 与 报警 系统
self-diagnosis and alarm system

diànkòng rányóu pēnshè EFI
E. 电控 燃油 喷射（EFI）
electronic fuel injection (EFI)

dàisù kòngzhì xìtǒng ISC
F. 怠速 控制 系统（ISC）
idle speed control (ISC) system

Diànkòng xìtǒng suǒ kòngzhì de nèiróng bāokuò:
电控 系统 所 控制 的 内容 包括：________
The content controlled by the electronic control system includes

二、课文 kèwén Texts

A 07-01

túdi: Shīfu, chējiān li de nà tái chē qǐdòng hòu dàisù shí fādòngjī yǒuxiē dǒudòng.
徒弟：师傅，车间里的那台车起动后怠速时发动机有些抖动。

shīfu: Wǒmen lái jiǎnchá yíxiàr fādòngjī de diànkòng xìtǒng.
师傅：我们来检查一下儿发动机的电控 系统。

túdi: Hǎo de, gùzhàng zhěnduànyí zhōng fādòngjī gùzhàngmǎ xiǎnshì dì 3 gāng diǎnhuǒ xiànquān gùzhàng.
徒弟：好的，故障诊断仪中发动机故障码显示第3缸点火线圈故障。

shīfu: Míngbai, nà jiù chángshì gēnghuàn yí gè xīn de diǎnhuǒ xiànquān língjiàn.
师傅：明白，那就尝试更换一个新的点火线圈零件。

túdi: Guǒrán, gēnghuàn guò língjiàn hòu xiǎnshì gùzhàng xiūfù. Xièxie shīfu.
徒弟：果然，更换过零件后显示故障修复。谢谢师傅。

译文 yìwén Text in English

Apprentice: Master, the engine of the vehicle in the workshop slightly shakes while idling after starting.
Master: Let's check the electronic control system of the engine.
Apprentice: OK. The engine fault code on the fault diagnosis instrument shows that the ignition coil of Cylinder 3 doesn't work.
Master: I see. Then try to replace it with a new ignition coil part.
Apprentice: As expected, it showed that the fault was corrected after replacing the part. Thank you, master.

普通词语 pǔtōng cíyǔ General Vocabulary

07-02

1.	那就	nà jiù	phr.	then
2.	尝试	chángshì	v.	try
3.	新	xīn	adj.	new
4.	果然	guǒrán	conj.	as expected

专业词语 zhuānyè cíyǔ Specialized Vocabulary

07-03

1.	怠速	dàisù	v.	idle
2.	抖动	dǒudòng	v.	shake
3.	电控系统	diànkòng xìtǒng	phr.	electronic control system
4.	故障码	gùzhàngmǎ	n.	fault code
5.	缸	gāng	n.	cylinder
6.	零件	língjiàn	n.	spare part(s)
7.	修复	xiūfù	v.	repair

启动系统

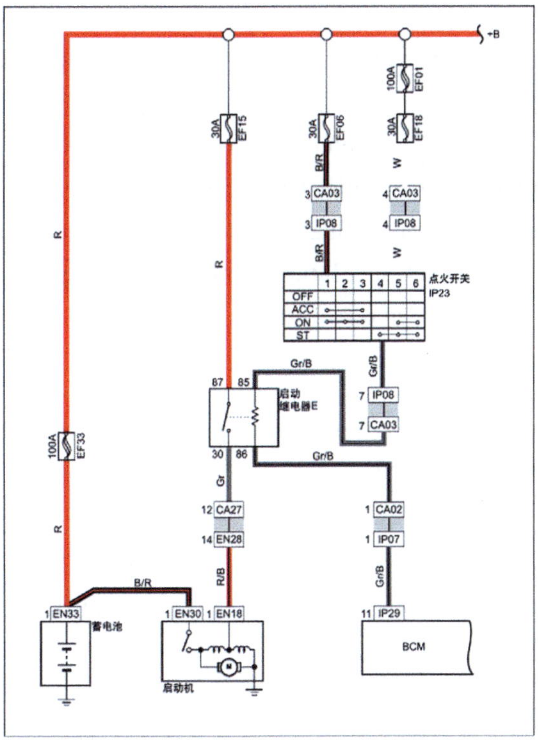

diànlùtú
电路图
circuit diagram

B 07-04

túdi: Shīfu, chējiān li yǒu tái chē shǐyòng yàoshi qǐdòng shí wú fǎnyìng, xùdiànchí diànyā zhèngcháng.
徒弟：师傅，车间里有台车使用钥匙起动时无反应，蓄电池电压正常。

shīfu: Háishi ànzhào guànlì, xiān shǐyòng gùzhàng zhěnduànyí dú yíxiàr gùzhàngmǎ.
师傅：还是按照惯例，先使用故障诊断仪读一下儿故障码。

túdi: Zhěnduànyí xiǎnshì fādòngjī qǐdòng xìnhào xiànlù duànlù.
徒弟：诊断仪显示发动机起动信号线路断路。

shīfu: Nà jiù jiéhé diànlùtú jiǎnchá yíxiàr xiāngguān de diànlù.
师傅：那就结合电路图检查一下儿相关的电路。

túdi: Gùzhàngdiǎn chádào le, yuánlái shì jìdiànqì méiyǒu ānzhuāng dàowèi, yǐjīng fùyuán le, gùzhàng jiěchú.
徒弟：故障点查到了，原来是继电器没有安装到位，已经复原了，故障解除。

译文 yìwén Text in English

Apprentice: Master, there is a vehicle in the workshop that cannot be started with the key. The storage battery voltage is normal.

Master: As usual, read the fault code with the fault diagnosis instrument.

Apprentice: The instrument displays that the engine start signal circuit is open.

Master: Then check the relevant circuits in combination with the circuit diagram.

Apprentice: The fault point has been indentified. It turned out that the relay was not installed in place. It has been restored. The fault has been removed.

普通词语 pǔtōng cíyǔ General Vocabulary

07-05

1.	钥匙	yàoshi	n.	key
2.	反应	fǎnyìng	n.	response
3.	惯例	guànlì	n.	convention
4.	结合	jiéhé	v.	combine
5.	相关	xiāngguān	v.	be related
6.	到位	dàowèi	v.	be in place

专业词语 zhuānyè cíyǔ Specialized Vocabulary

07-06

1.	故障点	gùzhàngdiǎn	n.	fault point
2.	复原	fùyuán	v.	restore
3.	解除	jiěchú	v.	remove

三、视听说 shì-tīng-shuō Viewing, Listening and Speaking

1. 观看介绍机油压力故障诊断相关视频，了解机油压力报警灯闪烁的故障检测步骤，将缺少的部分补充完整。**Watch the related video introducing the diagnosis of engine oil pressure faults, learn about the fault detection steps for the flashing engine oil pressure alarm lamp, and complete the missing parts.**

gùkè: Nín hǎo, wǒ chē de yíbiǎopán shang de (1) liàng le, zěnme bàn?
顾客：您好，我车的仪表盘上的（1）________亮了，怎么办？
Hello! The (1) ________ on the dashboard of my vehicle is on. What shall I do?

shīfu: Bié zháojí, wǒ xiān yòng (2) jiǎncè yíxià.
师傅：别着急，我先用（2）________检测一下。
Don't worry. I'll test it with (2) ________ first.

túdi: Shīfu, gěi nín. Shì shénme wèntí ne?
徒弟：师傅，给您。是什么问题呢？
Here you are, master. What's the problem?

shīfu: Shì (3) gùzhàng, wǒ chále xiànlù, méiyǒu wèntí. Kěnéng shì běntǐ gùzhàng, gēnghuàn yí gè xīn jiàn, shì yíxià.
师傅：是（3）________故障，我查了线路，没有问题。可能是本体故障，更换一个新件，试一下。
It is (3) ________ fault. I've checked the circuit and there is no problem with it. It may be a body fault. Try to replace it with a new one.

túdi: Shīfu, wǒ huànle yí gè xīn jiàn, gùzhàng jiěchú le.
徒弟：师傅，我换了一个新件，故障解除了。
Master, I've replaced it with a new one, and the fault has been removed.

jīyóu yālì bàojǐngqì
A. 机油压力报警器
engine oil pressure alarm

jīyóu yālì bàojǐngdēng
B. 机油压力报警灯
engine oil pressure alarm lamp

zhěnduànyí
C. 诊断仪
diagnosis instrument

2. 说一说 Let's talk

说说机油压力报警灯闪烁的故障检测步骤。

Talk about the fault detection steps for the flashing engine oil pressure alarm lamp.

四、学以致用 xuéyǐzhìyòng Practicing What You Have Learnt

观看介绍发动机转速为零故障诊断相关视频，将流程填在对应序号下的横线上，并说出工作流程。

Watch the related video introducing the diagnosis of zero engine speed faults, fill in the processes on the lines under the corresponding serial numbers, and tell the workflow.

gùzhàng zhěnduànyí jiǎncè
A. 故障 诊断仪 检测
detect with a fault diagnosis instrument

chājǐn xiànshù, gùzhàng xiūfù
B. 插紧 线束， 故障 修复
tighten the wire harness to remove the fault

fādòngjī zhuànsù wéi líng
C. 发动机 转速 为 零
the engine speed is zero

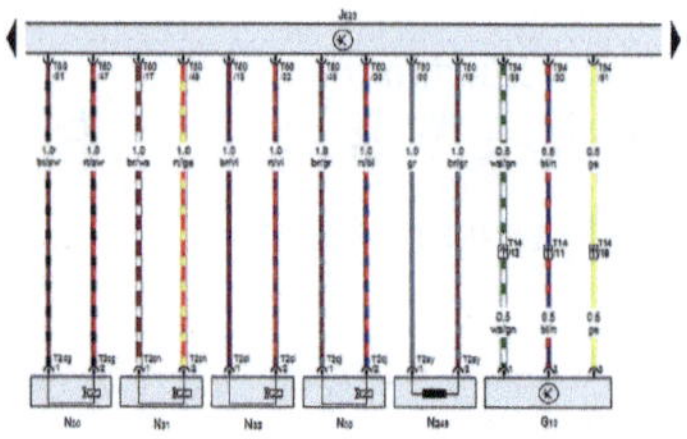

G28 zhuànsù chuángǎnqì dǎoxiàn duànlù
D. G28 转速 传感器 导线 断路
the G28 speed sensor wire is open.

1. ____ → 2. ____ → 3. ____ → 4. ____

五、小知识 xiǎo zhīshi Tips

Diànkòng fādòngjī
电控 发动机

Diànkòng fādòngjī yìngyòng xiàndài diànzǐ kòngzhì jìshù, tōngguò ānzhuāng chuángǎnqì huòqǔ
电控 发动机应用 现代电子控制技术，通过 安装 传感器获取

shùjù, jīngguò fādòngjī diànkòng dānyuán (ECU) yùnsuàn, jiāng xìnhào fāsòng gěi kòngzhì
数据，经过发动机电控 单元（ECU）运算，将信号发送给控制

zhíxíngqì, jīngquè kòngzhì fādòngjī de yùnxíng cānshù, gèngjiā jiénéng、gāoxiào, tígāole
执行器，精确控制发动机的运行 参数，更加节能、高效，提高了

fādòngjī de jīngjìxìng hé dònglìxìng, gǎishànle páifàng xìngnéng.
发动机的经济性和动力性，改善了排放 性能。

Electronic Control Engine

The electronic control engine applies modern electronic control technology, obtains data by installing sensors, and sends signals to the control actuator through the calculation of the engine electronic control unit (ECU), so as to accurately control the operating parameters of the engine, make it more energy-saving and efficient, improve its economical efficiency and power performance and improve its emission performance.

补充专业词语 bǔchōng zhuānyè cíyǔ Supplementary Specialized Vocabulary

07-07

1.	报警灯	bàojǐngdēng	n.	alarm lamp
2.	排放	páifàng	v.	emit

第二部分 Part 2

汉字 Chinese Characters

一、汉字知识 Hànzì zhīshi Knowledge about Chinese Characters

汉字的偏旁（7） **Radicals of Chinese characters (7)**

偏旁 Radicals	例字 Examples	部件组合 Combinations	结构图示 Illustrations
走	超	走+召	⿺
	趣	走+取	⿺
	起	走+己	⿺
	趟	走+尚	⿺
忄	忙	忄+亡	⿰
	快	忄+夬	⿰
	慢	忄+曼	⿰
	惯	忄+贯	⿰
	情	忄+青	⿰
攵	教	孝+攵	⿰
	收	丩+攵	⿰
	数	娄+攵	⿰
	放	方+攵	⿰
饣	馆	饣+官	⿰
	饭	饣+反	⿰
	饺	饣+交	⿰
	饼	饣+并	⿰
	饿	饣+我	⿰

偏旁 Radicals	例字 Examples	部件组合 Combinations	结构图示 Illustrations
禾	和	禾＋口	⿰
	种	禾＋中	⿰
	租	禾＋且	⿰
	季	禾＋子	⿱

二、汉字认读与书写 Hànzì rèndú yǔ shūxiě The Recognition and Writing of Chinese Characters

认读下列词语，并试着读写构成词语的汉字。**Recognize the following words, and try to read and write the Chinese characters forming these words.**

起动　惯例　失效　排放

起				动				惯				例			
失				效				排				放			

第三部分 Part 3 日常用语 *Daily Expressions*

1. 我们真诚地希望你们在这里过得愉快。Wǒmen zhēnchéng de xīwàng nǐmen zài zhèlǐ guò de yúkuài. We sincerely hope you'll have a pleasant stay here.
2. 质量比数量更重要。Zhìliàng bǐ shùliàng gèng zhòngyào. Quality is more important than quantity.

第四部分 Part 4 单元实训 *Unit Practical Training*

发动机电控系统常规检测
Routine Detection of Engine Electronic Control System

实训目的 Training purpose

通过本次实训，实训人员能够了解使用故障诊断仪读取发动机故障码的步骤。

Through the practical training, the trainees will be able to learn about the steps of reading engine fault codes with the fault diagnosis instrument.

实训步骤 Training steps

❶ 教师展示读取发动机故障码步骤的图片。

The teacher shows the pictures of the steps of reading engine fault codes.

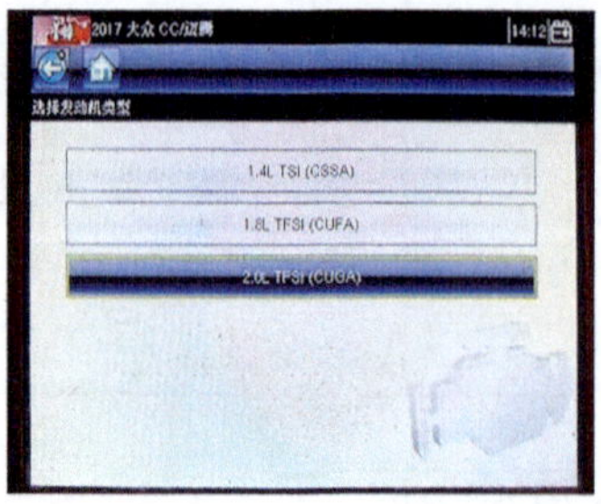

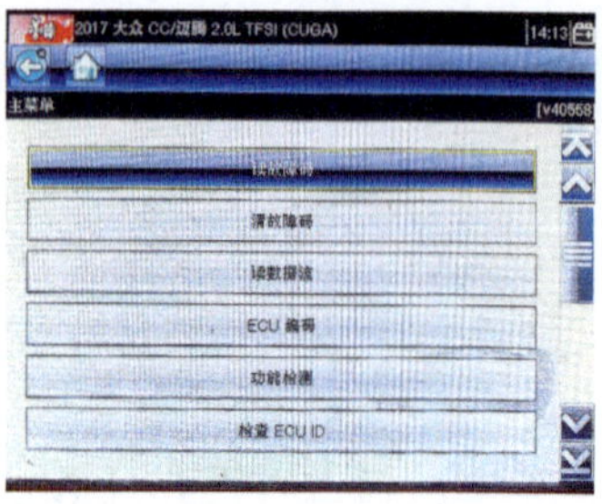

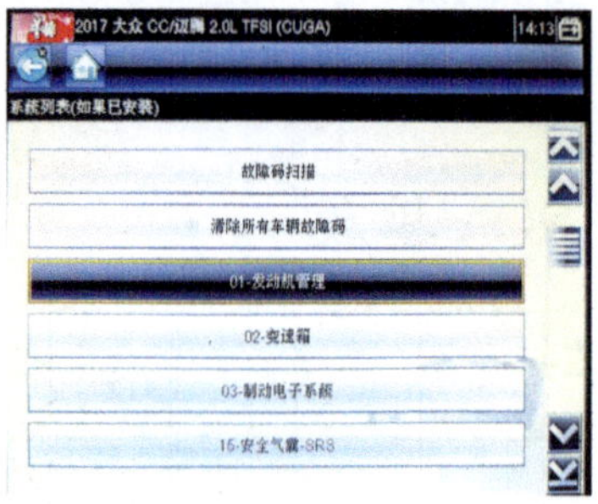

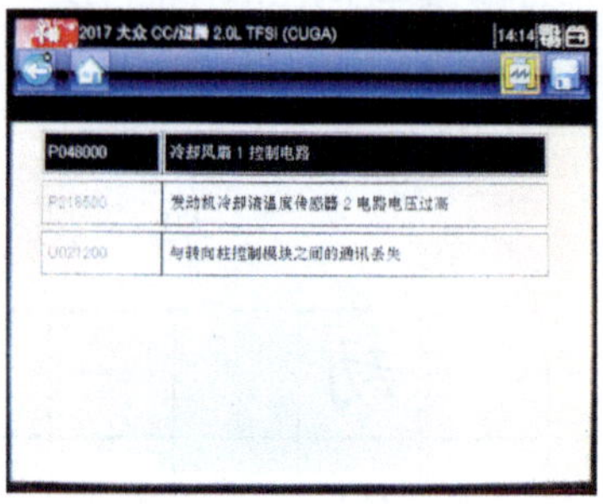

❷ 将实训人员分成若干小组，每组 3 ～ 5 人。

Divide the trainees into groups of 3-5.

❸ 学员分组讨论读取故障码的步骤顺序。

The trainees work in groups to discuss the sequence of the steps of reading fault codes.

❹ 抽取一个小组，展示小组结论，并给出步骤顺序。

Select a group to demonstrate their conclusions and provide the sequence of the steps.

❺ 教师总结评价，实训结束。

The teacher summarizes and evaluates, and the training ends.

第五部分 Part 5

单元小结 Unit Summary

cíyǔ
词语
Vocabulary

普通词语 General Vocabulary

1.	那就	nà jiù	phr.	then
2.	尝试	chángshì	v.	try
3.	新	xīn	adj.	new
4.	果然	guǒrán	conj.	as expected

cíyǔ
词语
Vocabulary

5.	钥匙	yàoshi	n.	key
6.	反应	fǎnyìng	n.	response
7.	惯例	guànlì	n.	convention
8.	结合	jiéhé	v.	combine
9.	相关	xiāngguān	v.	be related
10.	到位	dàowèi	v.	be in place

专业词语 Specialized Vocabulary

1.	怠速	dàisù	v.	idle
2.	抖动	dǒudòng	v.	shake
3.	电控系统	diànkòng xìtǒng	phr.	electronic control system
4.	故障码	gùzhàngmǎ	n.	fault code
5.	缸	gāng	n.	cylinder
6.	零件	língjiàn	n.	spare part(s)
7.	修复	xiūfù	v.	repair
8.	故障点	gùzhàngdiǎn	n.	fault point
9.	复原	fùyuán	v.	restore
10.	解除	jiěchú	v.	remove

补充专业词语 Supplementary Specialized Vocabulary

1.	报警灯	bàojǐngdēng	n.	alarm lamp
2.	排放	páifàng	v.	emit

jùzi
句子
Sentences

1. 故障诊断仪中发动机故障码显示第 3 缸点火线圈故障。
2. 还是按照惯例，先使用故障诊断仪读一下儿故障码。
3. 故障点查到了，原来是继电器没有安装到位，已经复原了，故障解除。

ABS gùzhàng zhěnduàn

ABS 故障诊断

ABS Fault Diagnosis

qìchē ABS gùzhàng jiǎncè bùzhòu

汽车 ABS 故障 检测 步骤

Steps of Automotive ABS Fault Detection

quèrèn gùzhàng xiànxiàng, chūbù jiǎnchá

确认 故障 现象，初步 检查

Confirm the Fault Phenomenon and Conduct Preliminary Inspection

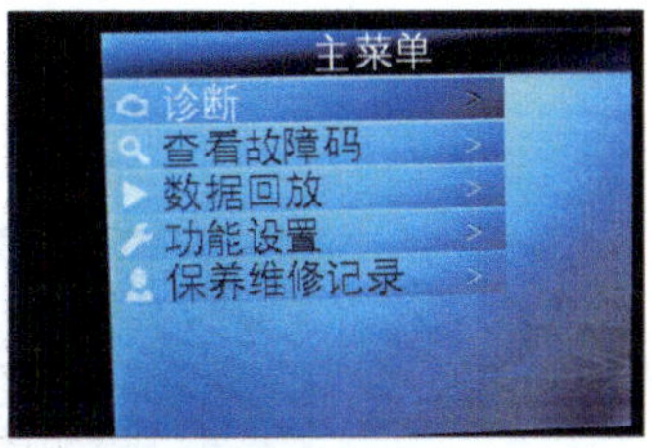

shǐyòng gùzhàng zhěnduànyí dú gùzhàngmǎ

使用 故障 诊断仪 读 故障码

Read the Fault Code with a Fault Diagnosis Instrument

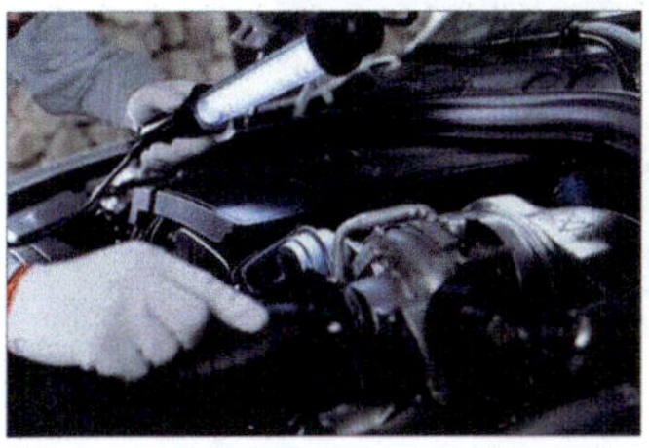

shǐyòng gōngjù、yíqì jìnxíng jiǎnchá, páichú gùzhàng

使用 工具、仪器 进行 检查，排除 故障

Use Tools and Instruments for Inspection and Troubleshooting

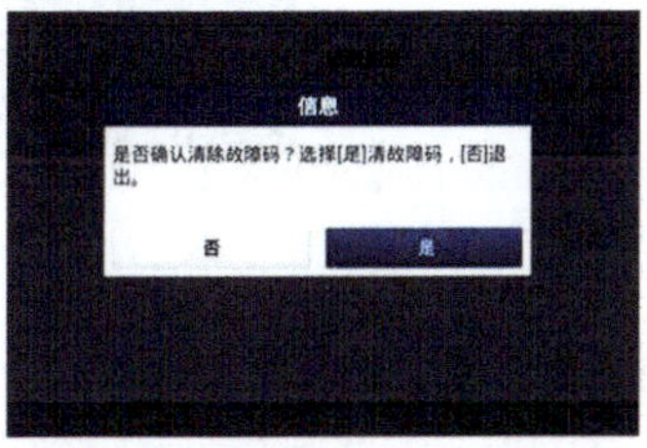

qīngchú gùzhàngmǎ bìng zài cì dúqǔ gùzhàngmǎ, quèrèn wú gùzhàngmǎ

清除 故障码 并 再 次读取 故障码，确认 无 故障码

Clear the Fault Code, and Read the Fault Code Again to Confirm That There Is No Fault Code

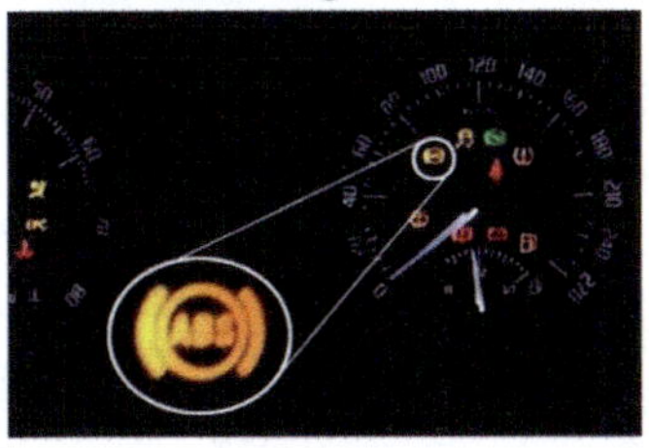

jiǎnchá ABS gùzhàng zhǐshìdēng zhuàngtài

检查ABS 故障 指示灯 状态

Check the Status of the ABS Fault Indicator Light

dāng ABS gùzhàng zhǐshìdēng bú zài shǎnshuò hòu, jìnxíng lùshì

当 ABS 故障 指示灯 不 再 闪烁 后，进行 路试

When the ABS Fault Indicator Light Does Not Flickern Any Longer, Conduct a Road Test

题解　Introduction

1. 学习内容：汽车 ABS 系统的组成，故障诊断工具和检测步骤。
   Learning content: The composition of automotive ABS system, fault diagnosis tools and detection steps
2. 知识目标：学习汽车 ABS 故障诊断的关键词和常用句型，学习汉字的偏旁和结构，学写相关汉字。
   Knowledge objectives: To learn the keywords and common sentence patterns for automotive ABS fault diagnosis, learn the radicals and structures of Chinese characters, and learn to write the related Chinese characters
3. 技能目标：掌握 ABS 故障诊断的操作方法。
   Skill objective: To master the operation method of ABS fault diagnosis

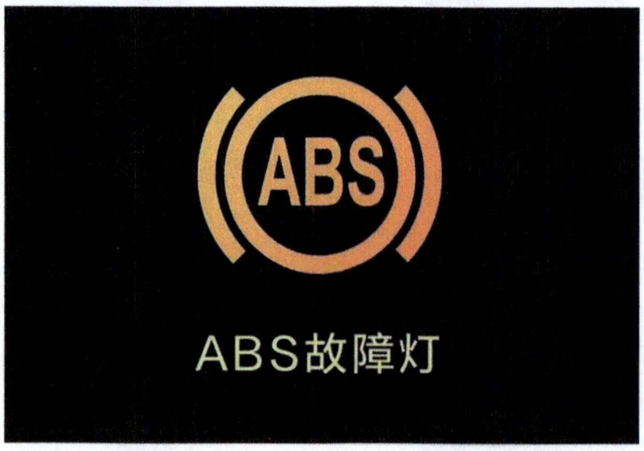

第一部分　Part 1

课文　Texts

一、热身　rèshēn　Warm-up

1. 给词语选择对应的图片。**Choose the corresponding pictures for the words.**

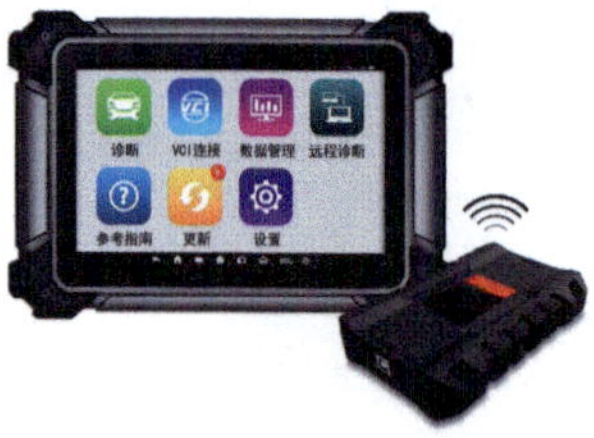

A.

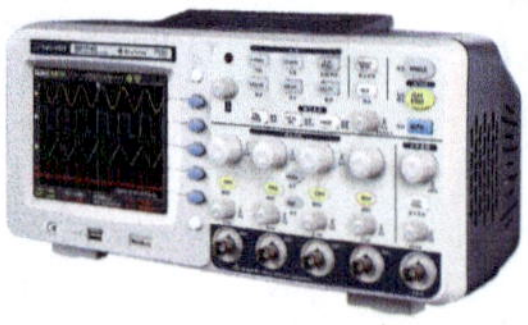

B.

C.

D.

① wànyòngbiǎo 万用表 ____________ multimeter

② shìbōqì 示波器 ____________ oscilloscope

fángbàosǐ zhìdòng xìtǒng zhǐshìdēng
③ 防抱死 制动 系统 指示灯 ____________
Anti-lock Braking System (ABS) indicator lamp

gùzhàng zhěnduànyí
④ 故障 诊断仪 ____________
fault diagnosis instrument

2. 观看介绍 ABS 系统相关视频，了解汽车 ABS 系统，并选出 ABS 的作用。**Watch the related video introducing the ABS system, learn about it, and choose the functions of ABS.**

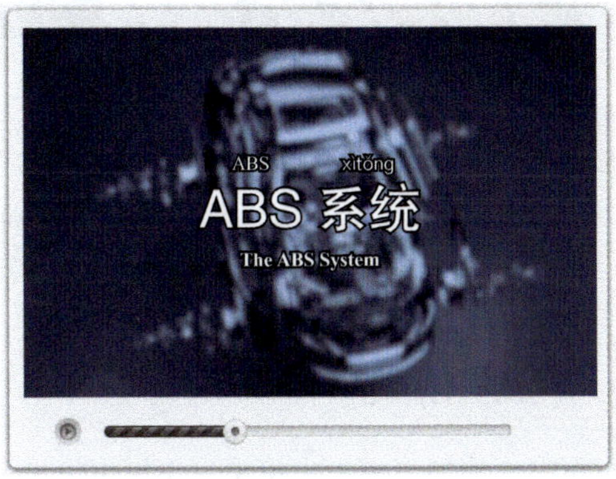

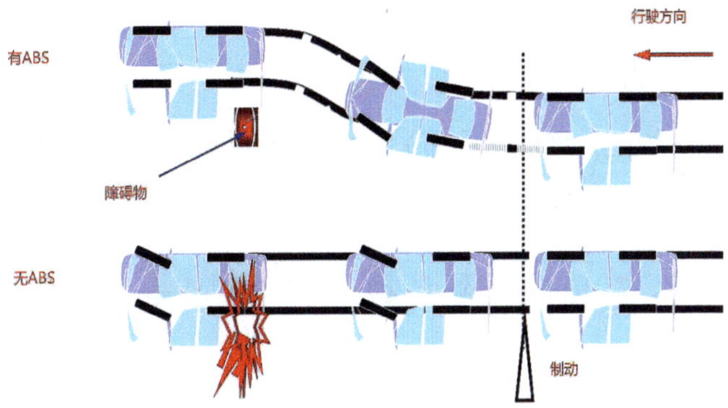

Bǎozhèng qìchē de xíngshǐ ānquán.
① 保证汽车的行驶安全。 (　　)
Ensure the driving safety of the car.

Tígāo zhìdòng jiǎnsùdù.
② 提高制动减速度。 (　　)
Increase the braking deceleration.

Zēngjiā lúntāi mósǔn.
③ 增加轮胎磨损。 (　　)
Increase tire wear.

Tígāo qìchē fāngxiàng de wěndìngxìng hé zhuǎnxiàng cāozòng nénglì.
④ 提高汽车方向的稳定性和转向操纵能力。 (　　)
Improve the directional stability and steering control ability of the car.

Suōduǎn zhìdòng jùlí.
⑤ 缩短制动距离。 (　　)
Shorten the braking distance.

二、课文 kèwén Texts

A 08-01

túdi: Shīfu, zhè liàng chē de fángbàosǐ zhìdòng xìtǒng chūxiànle gùzhàng.
徒弟：师傅，这辆车的防抱死制动系统出现了故障。

shīfu: Chūbù jiǎnchále ma? Shì shénme qíngkuàng?
师傅：初步检查了吗？是什么情况？

túdi: Yíbiǎopán de ABS gùzhàngdēng shǎnshuò, bìng yǒu gùzhàng tíshì, jǐnjí zhìdòng shí chēlún bèi bàosǐ, bìngqiě dǎhuá.
徒弟：仪表盘的ABS故障灯闪烁，并有故障提示，紧急制动时车轮被抱死，并且打滑。

shīfu: Hǎo de, xiān quèdìng gùzhàng yuányīn. Nǐ xiān zhǔnbèi jiǎncè yòng de gōngjù ba.
师傅：好的，先确定故障原因。你先准备检测用的工具吧。

túdi: Shīfu, wǒ zhǔnbèile gùzhàng zhěnduànyí、shìbōqì hé wànyòngbiǎo.
徒弟：师傅，我准备了故障诊断仪、示波器和万用表。

shīfu: Fēicháng hǎo.
师傅：非常好。

译文 yìwén Text in English

Apprentice: Master, the anti-lock braking system of this vehicle has failed.

Master: Have you had a preliminary check? What's going on?

Apprentice: The ABS fault light on the dashboard flickers with a fault prompt. During emergency braking, the wheels are locked and skidding.

Master: Alright. Let's determine the cause of the fault first. Please prepare detection tools.

Apprentice: Master, I've prepared a fault diagnosis instrument, an oscilloscope and a multimeter.

Master: Very good.

普通词语 pǔtōng cíyǔ General Vocabulary 08-02

1.	初步	chūbù	adj.	preliminary
2.	紧急	jǐnjí	adj.	urgent

专业词语 zhuānyè cíyǔ Specialized Vocabulary

08-03

1.	防抱死制动系统	fángbàosǐ zhìdòng xìtǒng	phr.	anti-lock braking system
2.	故障灯	gùzhàngdēng	n.	fault light
3.	提示	tíshì	v.	prompt
4.	抱死	bàosǐ	v.	lock
5.	打滑	dǎhuá	v.	skid

B 08-04

shīfu: Liánjiē gùzhàng zhěnduànyí dúqǔ yíxiàr ABS gùzhàngmǎ.
师傅：连接故障诊断仪读取一下儿ABS故障码。

túdi: Hǎo de. Gùzhàng zhěnduànyí xiǎnshì zuǒhòulún lúnsù chuángǎnqì xiànlù gùzhàng.
徒弟：好的。故障诊断仪显示左后轮轮速传感器线路故障。

shīfu: Yòng wànyòngbiǎo cèliáng yíxiàr zhège chuángǎnqì de xiànlù liánjiē shìfǒu zhèngcháng.
师傅：用万用表测量一下儿这个传感器的线路连接是否正常。

túdi: Shīfu, wǒ fāxiàn qízhōng yì gēn dǎoxiàn pòsǔn, dǎozhì duànlù, xiànzài yǐjīng xiūfù hǎo le.
徒弟：师傅，我发现其中一根导线破损，导致断路，现在已经修复好了。

shīfu: Hǎo de, zài yòng shìbōqì cǎijí chuángǎnqì bōxíng, quèbǎo chuángǎnqì gōngzuò zhèngcháng. Zuìhòu zài yòng gùzhàng zhěnduànyí, qīngchú lìshǐ gùzhàng bìng zàicì dúqǔ gùzhàngmǎ.
师傅：好的，再用示波器采集传感器波形，确保传感器工作正常。最后再用故障诊断仪，清除历史故障并再次读取故障码。

译文 yìwén Text in English

Master: Connect the fault diagnosis instrument to read the fault code of ABS.

Apprentice: OK. The fault diagnosis instrument shows a faulty left rear wheel speed sensor circuit.

Master: Use the multimeter to measure whether the circuit connection of this sensor is normal.

Apprentice: Master, I found that one of the wires was damaged, resulting in an open circuit. Now I've repaired it.

Master: OK. Then use the oscilloscope to collect the sensor waveform to ensure that the sensor works normally. Finally, use the fault diagnosis instrument to clear past faults and read the fault code again.

gùzhàng zhěnduànyí
① 故障 诊断仪
fault diagnosis instrument

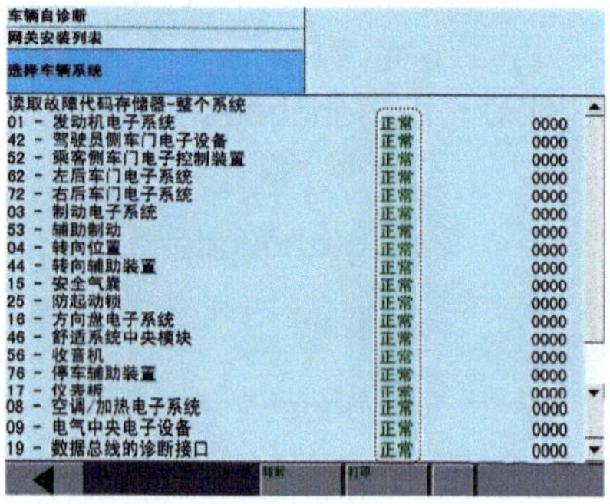

gùzhàngmǎ
② 故障码
fault code

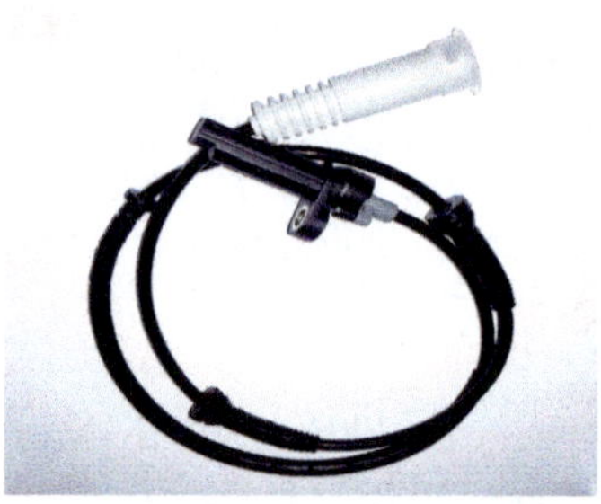

lúnsù chuángǎnqì
③ 轮速 传感器
wheel speed sensor

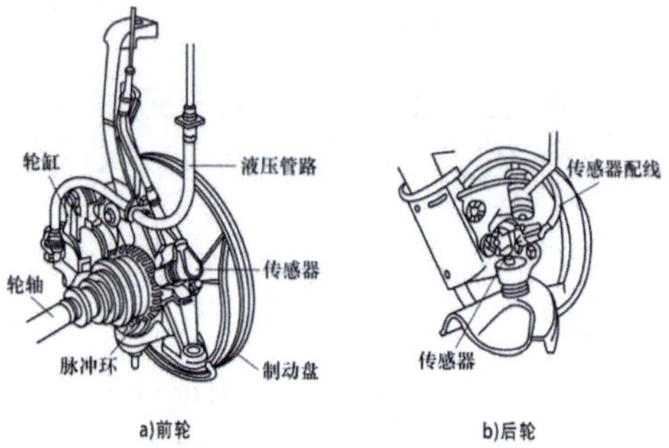

lúnsù chuángǎnqì ānzhuāng wèizhì
④ 轮速 传感器 安装 位置
mounting position of a wheel speed sensor

普通词语 pǔtōng cíyǔ General Vocabulary

08-05

1.	破损	pòsǔn	v.	damage
2.	导致	dǎozhì	v.	result in
3.	确保	quèbǎo	v.	ensure
4.	清除	qīngchú	v.	clear
5.	历史	lìshǐ	n.	one's past/record
6.	再次	zàicì	adv.	again

专业词语 zhuānyè cíyǔ Specialized Vocabulary

08-06

1.	轮速传感器	lúnsù chuángǎnqì	phr.	wheel speed sensor
2.	采集	cǎijí	v.	collect

三、视听说 shì-tīng-shuō Viewing, Listening and Speaking

1. 观看介绍 ABS 系统组成部分相关视频，将 ABS 系统的主要组成部分与其功能连线。Watch the related video introducing the components of the ABS system and connect the main components of the ABS system with their functions.

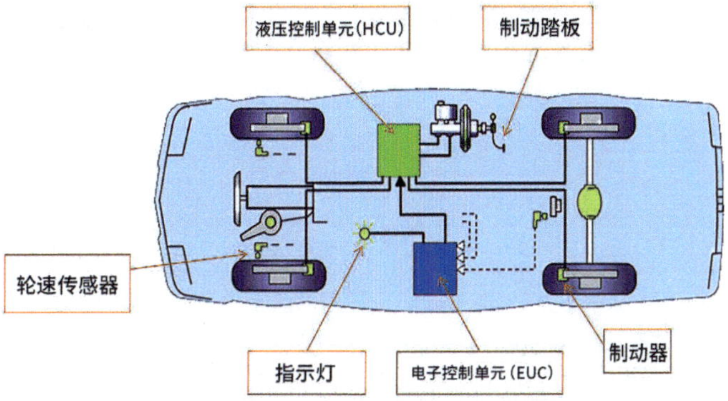

lúnsù chuángǎnqì ❶ 轮速 传感器 wheel speed sensor	shūchū kòngzhì zhǐlìng A. 输出 控制 指令 output control instructions
	jiǎncè chēlún zhuànsù B. 检测 车轮 转速 detect wheel speed
diànzǐ kòngzhì dānyuán ❷ 电子 控制 单元 electronic control unit (ECU)	jiēshōu ECU de zhǐlìng C. 接收 ECU 的 指令 receive instructions from ECU
	jiēshōu xìnhào D. 接收 信号 receive signals
yèyā kòngzhì dānyuán ❸ 液压 控制 单元 hydraulic control unit (HCU)	kòngzhì zhìdòng yālì tiáojiéqì E. 控制 制动 压力 调节器 control brake pressure regulator
	tígōng xìnhào gěi ECU F. 提供 信号 给 ECU provide signals to ECU

2. 说一说 **Let's talk**

说说 ABS 系统的组成。**Talk about the components of the ABS system.**

四、学以致用 xuéyǐzhìyòng Practicing What You Have Learnt

观看介绍 ABS 系统故障诊断相关视频，了解 ABS 系统故障诊断步骤，并将以下步骤排序。**Watch the related video introducing ABS system fault diagnosis, learn about the steps of ABS system fault diagnosis, and sort them out.**

Qīngchú gùzhàngmǎ.
A. 清除故障码。
Clear the fault code.

Quèrèn gùzhàng qíngkuàng, chūbù jiǎnchá.
B. 确认故障情况，初步检查。
Confirm the fault situation and conduct preliminary inspection.

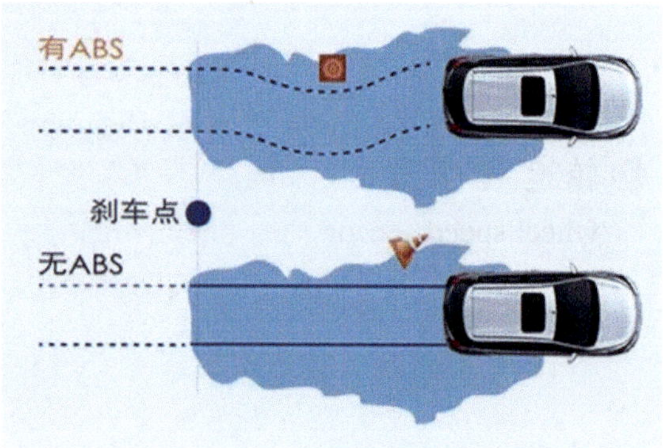

Jiǎnchá ABS zhǐshìdēng zhuàngtài.
C. 检查 ABS 指示灯状态。
Check the status of ABS indicator light.

Lìyòng gùzhàng zhěnduànyí dúqǔ gùzhàngmǎ.
D. 利用故障诊断仪读取故障码。
Read the fault code with a fault diagnosis instrument.

Jìnxíng lùshì.
E. 进行路试。
Carry out a road test.

Lìyòng gōngjù jìnxíng shēnrù jiǎnchá, páichú gùzhàng.
F. 利用工具进行深入检查，排除故障。
Use tools for in-depth inspection and troubleshooting.

五、小知识 xiǎo zhīshi Tips

ABS Xìtǒng de qiánshì jīnshēng
ABS 系统的前世今生

ABS de lìshǐ kěyǐ zhuīsù dào 20 shìjì 50 niándài. 1953 nián Méisàidésī – Bēnchí gōngchéngshī Hans Scherenberg shǒucì tíchū fángzhǐ chēlún zài zhìdòng shí bàosǐ de zhuānlì shēnqǐng, cǐhòu búduàn tóurù yánjiū, zhídào 1978 nián 8 yuè 22 rì zhì 25 rì, Méisàidésī-Bēnchí yǔ Bóshì zài Déguó Sītújiātè fābùle quánqiú shǒukuǎn ABS, bìngqiě shuàixiān yìngyòng yú W116 shìdài de S jí jiàochē.

ABS的历史可以追溯到20世纪50年代。1953年梅赛德斯–奔驰工程师Hans Scherenberg首次提出防止车轮在制动时抱死的专利申请，此后不断投入研究，直到1978年8月22日至25日，梅赛德斯-奔驰与博世在德国斯图加特发布了全球首款ABS，并且率先应用于W116世代的S级轿车。

Xiàndài qìchē ānzhuāng yǒu fángbàosǐ zhìdòng xìtǒng, ABS jì yǒu pǔtōng zhìdòng xìtǒng de zhìdòng gōngnéng, yòu néng fángzhǐ chēlún bàosǐ, shǐ qìchē zài zhìdòng zhuàngtài xià réng néng zhuǎnxiàng, bǎozhèng qìchē zhìdòng fāngxiàng de wěndìngxìng, fángzhǐ chǎnshēng cèhuá hé pǎopiān, shì zhìdòng xiàoguǒ jiào hǎo de zhìdòng zhuāngzhì.

现代汽车安装有防抱死制动系统，ABS既有普通制动系统的制动功能，又能防止车轮抱死，使汽车在制动状态下仍能转向，保证汽车制动方向的稳定性，防止产生侧滑和跑偏，是制动效果较好的制动装置。

Past and Present of the ABS System

The history of ABS can be traced back to the 1950s. In 1953, Hans Scherenberg, an engineer of Mercedes-Benz, first applied for a patent to prevent the wheels from being locked during braking. Since then, more research has been carried out. During August 22-25, 1978, Mercedes-Benz and Bosch released the first ABS in the world in Stuttgart, Germany, and took the lead in applying it to the W116 S-class sedans.

Anti-lock braking systems are installed on modern vehicles. ABS not only has the braking function of an ordinary braking system, but also can prevent the wheels from being locked, so that the vehicle can still turn in the braking state, which ensures the braking directional stability of the vehicle and prevents side-slip and deviation. It is a braking device with good braking effect.

补充专业词语 bǔchōng zhuānyè cíyǔ Supplementary Specialized Vocabulary

08-07

1.	电子控制单元	diànzǐ kòngzhì dānyuán	phr.	electronic control unit
2.	液压控制单元	yèyā kòngzhì dānyuán	phr.	hydraulic control unit
3.	指令	zhǐlìng	n.	instruction
4.	制动压力调节器	zhìdòng yālì tiáojiéqì	phr.	brake pressure regulator
5.	轿车	jiàochē	n.	sedan
6.	侧滑	cèhuá	v.	side skidding
7.	跑偏	pǎopiān	v.	deviate

第二部分 Part 2

汉字 Chinese Characters

一、汉字知识 Hànzì zhīshi Knowledge about Chinese Characters

汉字的偏旁（8） **Radicals of Chinese characters (8)**

偏旁 Radicals	例字 Examples	部件组合 Combinations	结构图示 Illustrations
门	问	门＋口	
	闻	门＋耳	
	间	门＋日	
	闹	门＋市	
疒	病	疒＋丙	
	瘦	疒＋叟	
冂	网	冂＋㸚	
	同	冂＋𠮛	
	冈	冂＋㐅	
车	辆	车＋两	
	轻	车＋圣	
	较	车＋交	
	辅	车＋甫	

（续表）

偏旁 Radicals	例字 Examples	部件组合 Combinations	结构图示 Illustrations
贝	费	弗 + 贝	⊟
	赛	寒 + 贝	⊟
	贵	𠀐 + 贝	⊟

二、汉字认读与书写　Hànzì rèndú yǔ shūxiě　The Recognition and Writing of Chinese Characters

认读下列词语，并试着读写构成词语的汉字。**Recognize the following words, and try to read and write the Chinese characters forming these words.**

轮速　车间　电网　内饰　车辆

轮				速				车				间			
电				网				内				饰			
车				辆											

第三部分　Part 3

日常用语　*Daily Expressions*

1. 我想也许将来我们可以合作。Wǒ xiǎng yěxǔ jiānglái wǒmen kěyǐ hézuò. I think we may be able to work together in the future.
2. 我们想把生意扩大到中国市场。Wǒmen xiǎng bǎ shēngyi kuòdà dào Zhōngguó shìchǎng. We are thinking of expanding our business into the Chinese market.

第四部分　Part 4

单元实训　*Unit Practical Training*

ABS 故障检测 ABS Fault Detection

实训目的 Training purpose

通过本次实训，实训人员能够熟悉 ABS 故障检测的一般步骤。

Through the practical training, the trainees will be able to be familiar with the general steps of ABS fault detection.

实训步骤 Training steps

1. 教师准备 ABS 故障车辆与相关检测工具。
   The teacher prepares vehicles with ABS faults and related detection tools.
2. 教师讲解并演示 ABS 故障检测的一般步骤。
   The teacher explains and demonstrates the general steps of ABS fault detection.
3. 学员分组，每组 3 ～ 5 人。
   Divide the trainees into groups of 3-5.
4. 学员正确使用工具，检测 ABS 故障，修复故障并进行验证。
   The trainees use tools correctly to detect ABS faults, repair and verify the faults.
5. 小组讨论，编写报告。
   Carry out a group discussion and write a report.
6. 教师总结评价，实训结束。
   The teacher summarizes and evaluates, and the training ends.

第五部分 Part 5

单元小结 Unit Summary

cíyǔ
词语
Vocabulary

普通词语 General Vocabulary

1.	初步	chūbù	adj.	preliminary
2.	紧急	jǐnjí	adj.	urgent
3.	破损	pòsǔn	v.	damage
4.	导致	dǎozhì	v.	result in
5.	确保	quèbǎo	v.	ensure
6.	清除	qīngchú	v.	clear
7.	历史	lìshǐ	n.	one's past/record
8.	再次	zàicì	adv.	again

专业词语 Specialized Vocabulary

1.	防抱死制动系统	fángbàosǐ zhìdòng xìtǒng	phr.	anti-lock braking system
2.	故障灯	gùzhàngdēng	n.	fault light
3.	提示	tíshì	v.	prompt
4.	抱死	bàosǐ	v.	lock
5.	打滑	dǎhuá	v.	skid

cíyǔ
词语
Vocabulary

6.	轮速传感器	lúnsù chuángǎnqì	phr.	wheel speed sensor
7.	采集	cǎijí	v.	collect

补充专业词语 Supplementary Specialized Vocabulary

1.	电子控制单元	diànzǐ kòngzhì dānyuán	phr.	electronic control unit
2.	液压控制单元	yèyā kòngzhì dānyuán	phr.	hydraulic control unit
3.	指令	zhǐlìng	n.	instruction
4.	制动压力调节器	zhìdòng yālì tiáojiéqì	phr.	brake pressure regulator
5.	轿车	jiàochē	n.	sedan
6.	侧滑	cèhuá	v.	side skidding
7.	跑偏	pǎopiān	v.	deviate

jùzǐ
句子
Sentences

1. 仪表盘的 ABS 故障灯闪烁，并有故障提示，紧急制动时车轮被抱死，并且打滑。
2. 连接故障诊断仪读取一下儿 ABS 故障码。
3. 用万用表测量一下儿这个传感器的线路连接是否正常。
4. 用示波器采集传感器波形，确保传感器工作正常。最后再用故障诊断仪，清除历史故障并再次读取故障码。

9

Qìchē qiánzhàodēng jiǎncè

汽车前照灯检测

Vehicle Headlamp Detection

qìchē qiánzhàodēng jiǎncè bùzhòu

汽车 前照灯 检测 步骤

Steps of Vehicle Headlamp Detection

dǎkāi dēngguāng kāiguān, jìlù gùzhàng xiànxiàng

打开 灯光 开关，记录 故障 现象

Turn on the Light Switch and Record the Fault Phenomenon

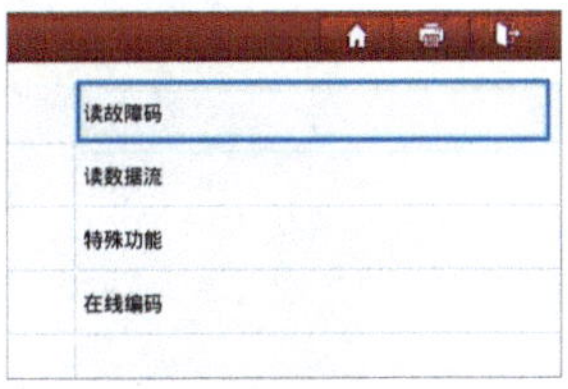

liánjiē gùzhàng zhěnduànyí, dúqǔ gùzhàngmǎ

连接 故障 诊断仪，读取 故障码

Connect the Fault Diagnosis Instrument to Read the Fault Code

suǒdìng gùzhàngdiǎn

锁定 故障点

Locate the Fault Point

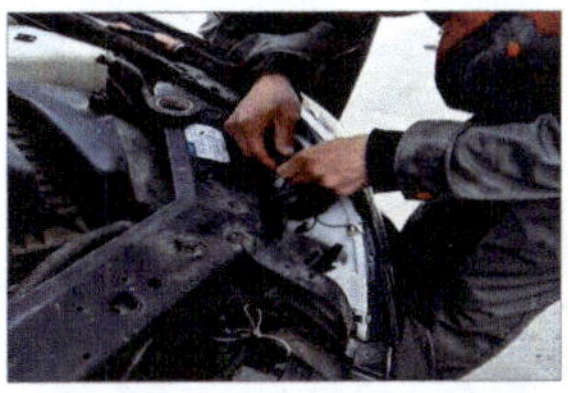

jiǎncè xiāngguān bùjiàn jí xiànshù

检测 相关 部件及线束

Detect the Relevant Parts and Wiring Harnesses

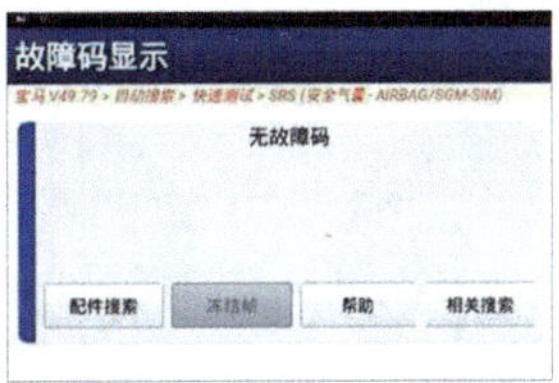

qīngchú gùzhàngmǎ bìng zàicì dúqǔ gùzhàngmǎ,

清除 故障码 并 再次读取故障码，

quèrèn wú gùzhàngmǎ

确认 无 故障码

Clear the Fault Code and Read It Again to Confirm There Is No Fault Code

xiūfù gùzhàng bìng yànzhèng

修复 故障 并 验证

dēngguāng xiàoguǒ

灯光 效果

Repair the Fault and Verify the Lighting Effect

题解 Introduction

1. 学习内容：汽车前照灯的组成与一般故障检测步骤。
   Learning content: The composition and general fault detection steps of vehicle headlamps
2. 知识目标：学习汽车前照灯故障检测的关键词和常用句型，学习汉字的偏旁和结构，学写相关汉字。
   Knowledge objectives: To learn the keywords and common sentence patterns for detecting faults in vehicle headlamps, learn the radicals and structures of Chinese characters, and learn to write the related Chinese characters
3. 技能目标：掌握汽车前照灯故障检测的操作方法。
   Skill objective: To master the operation method of vehicle headlamp fault detection

第一部分 Part 1

课文 Texts

一、热身 rèshēn Warm-up

1. 给词语选择对应的图片。**Choose the corresponding pictures for the words.**

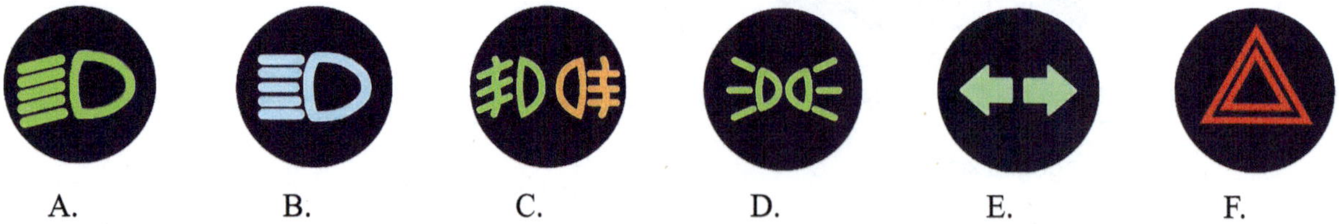

① wùdēng 雾灯 ______________ fog lamp

② yuǎnguāngdēng 远光灯 ______________ high beam

shìkuòdēng
③ 示廓灯 ________________
outline marker lamp

zhuǎnxiàngdēng
④ 转向灯 ________________
turn signal

jìnguāngdēng
⑤ 近光灯 ________________
low beam

wēixiǎn jǐngbàodēng
⑥ 危险警报灯 ________________
hazard warning signal

2. 观看介绍前照灯检测步骤相关视频，将下列步骤排序。**Watch the related video introducing the steps of headlamp detection and sort them out.**

Jiāng chēliàng xíngshǐ zhì guīdìng wèizhì.
A. 将车辆行驶至规定位置。
Drive the vehicle to the specified position.

Jiǎncè ruǎnjiàn fāchū zhǐlìng, jiǎncèyí cèliáng yuǎnguāngdēng.
B. 检测软件发出指令，检测仪测量远光灯。
The detection software gives instructions, and the detector measures the high beams.

Zhì biànsùqì yú kōngdǎng, chēliàng diànyuán chǔyú chōngdiàn zhuàngtài, kāiqǐ yuǎnguāngdēng.
C. 置变速器于空挡，车辆电源处于充电状态，开启远光灯。
Put the transmission in neutral gear, keep the vehicle power supply in the charging mode, and turn on the high beams.

Zhuǎnhuàn wéi jìnguāngdēng bìng jiǎncè.
D. 转换 为 近光灯 并检测。
Switch to the low beams and detect them.

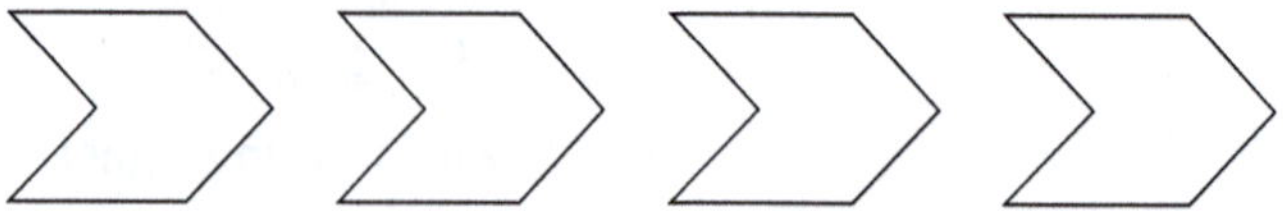

二、课文 kèwén Texts

A 09-01

kèhù jīnglǐ: Nǐ hǎo, zhè liàng chē de qiánzhàodēng yǒu gùzhàng, xūyào wéixiū.
客户经理：你好，这辆车的前照灯有故障，需要维修。

wéixiūgōng: Xiànzài yǒudiǎnr máng, nǐ xiān hé wǒ shuōshuo dàzhì qíngkuàng.
维修工：现在有点儿忙，你先和我说说大致情况。

kèhù jīnglǐ: Kèhù fǎnyìng dǎkāi jìnguāngdēng kāiguān, zuǒ yòu liàngdù yíyàng, dànshì dǎkāi yuǎnguāngdēng kāiguān, yòubian méiyǒu zuǒbian liàng.
客户经理：客户反映打开近光灯开关，左右亮度一样，但是打开远光灯开关，右边没有左边亮。

wéixiūgōng: Zhè yīnggāi shì yòu qián yuǎnguāngdēng yǒu wèntí.
维修工：这应该是右前远光灯有问题。

kèhù jīnglǐ: Shìde, máfan nǐ jiǎncè yíxiàr jùtǐ yuányīn, bāng kèhù xiūhǎo.
客户经理：是的，麻烦你检测一下儿具体原因，帮客户修好。

wéixiūgōng: Méi wèntí, wǒ shāohòu jiù chǔlǐ.
维修工：没问题，我稍后就处理。

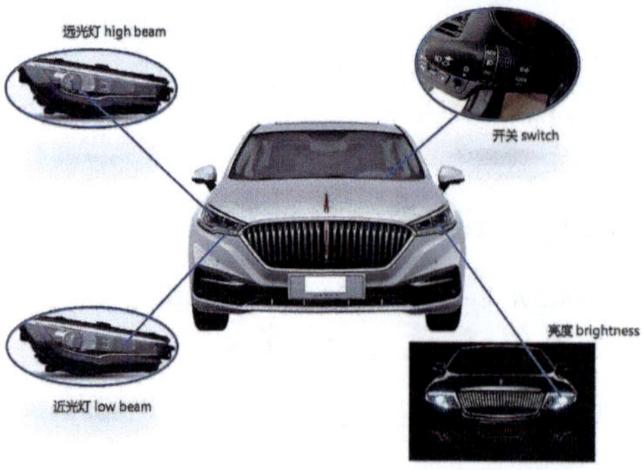

译文 yìwén Text in English

Customer Manager: Hello! The headlamps of this vehicle are malfunctioning and need to be repaired.
Maintenance Technician: I'm kind of busy now. Tell me the general situation first.

Customer Manager: The customer said that when the low beam switch was turned on, the left one and right one were of the same brightness. But when the high beam switch was turned on, the right one was not as bright as the left one.

Maintenance Technician: There should be a problem with the right front high beam.

Customer manager: Yes. Could you please check the specific reason and help the customer fix it?

Maintenance Technician: No problem. I'll deal with it later.

普通词语 pǔtōng cíyǔ General Vocabulary

09-02

1.	大致	dàzhì	adj.	general
2.	反映	fǎnyìng	v.	report, make known
3.	亮	liàng	adj.	bright
4.	原因	yuányīn	n.	reason
5.	没问题	méi wèntí	phr.	no problem
6.	稍后	shāohòu	adv.	later
7.	处理	chǔlǐ	v.	deal with

专业词语 zhuānyè cíyǔ Specialized Vocabulary

09-03

1.	近光灯	jìnguāngdēng	n.	low beam
2.	开关	kāiguān	n.	switch
3.	亮度	liàngdù	n.	brightness
4.	远光灯	yuǎnguāngdēng	n.	high beam

B

09-04

túdí: Shīfu, zhè liàng chē de qiánzhàodēng quèshí yǒu gùzhàng, gùzhàng zhěnduànyí dúqǔle gùzhàngmǎ.
徒弟：师傅，这辆车的前照灯确实有故障，故障诊断仪读取了故障码。

wéixiūgōng: Zuǒ、yòu jìnguāngdēng zhèngcháng, shuōmíng diànyuán、kòngzhìqì hé kāiguān dōu méiyǒu wèntí. Nà gùzhàngdiǎn kěnéng zài nǎli?
维修工：左、右近光灯正常，说明电源、控制器和开关都没有问题。那故障点可能在哪里？

túdí: Shīfu, shì jìdiànqì、bǎoxiǎnsī、dēngpào huòzhě dǎoxiàn ma?
徒弟：师傅，是继电器、保险丝、灯泡或者导线吗？

wéixiūgōng: Méi cuò. Nǐ bǎ wànyòngbiǎo ná guolai, xiān cèliáng yòu qián yuǎnguāngdēng de
维修工：没错。你把万用表拿过来，先测量右前远光灯的

bǎoxiǎnsī diànzǔ.
保险丝电阻。

túdi: Shīfu, bǎoxiǎnsī diànzǔ wúqióngdà.
徒弟：师傅，保险丝电阻无穷大。

wéixiūgōng: Nà jiù shì bǎoxiǎnsī huài le, dǎozhì xìtǒng duànlù. Gēnghuàn xīn de bǎoxiǎnsī, yīnggāi huì huīfù zhèngcháng.
维修工：那就是保险丝坏了，导致系统断路。更换新的保险丝，应该会恢复正常。

jìdiànqì
继电器
relay

bǎoxiǎnsī
保险丝
fuse

dēngpào
灯泡
bulb

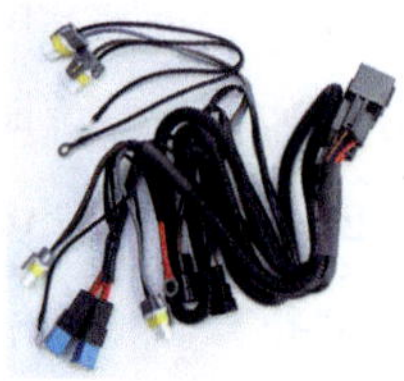

xiànshù
线束
wire harness

译文 yìwén Text in English

Apprentice: Master, the headlamps of this vehicle do have a problem. The fault diagnosis instrument has read the fault code.

Maintenance Technician: The left and right low beams are normal, indicating that there is no problem with the power supply, controller and switch. Where may the fault point be?

Apprentice: Master, may it be the relay, fuse, bulb or wire?

Maintenance Technician: That's right. Bring the multimeter and measure the fuse resistance of the right front high beam first.

Apprentice: Master, the fuse resistance value is infinite.

Maintenance Technician: The fuse is broken, resulting in an open circuit in the system. Replace the fuse with a new one and it should return to normal.

普通词语 pǔtōng cíyǔ General Vocabulary

09-05

1.	确实	quèshí	adv.	indeed
2.	应该	yīnggāi	aux.	should
3.	恢复	huīfù	v.	return to normal

专业词语 zhuānyè cíyǔ Specialized Vocabulary

09-06

1.	电源	diànyuán	n.	power supply
2.	控制器	kòngzhìqì	n.	controller

3. 灯泡	dēngpào	n.	bulb
4. 电阻	diànzǔ	n.	resistance, resistor
5. 无穷大	wúqióngdà	n.	infinity

三、视听说 shì-tīng-shuō Viewing, Listening and Speaking

1. 观看介绍汽车前照灯组成相关视频，了解汽车前照灯的组成，然后将下列句子补充完整。**Watch the related video introducing the components of an automobile headlamp, learn about the components of an automobile headlamp and complete the following sentences.**

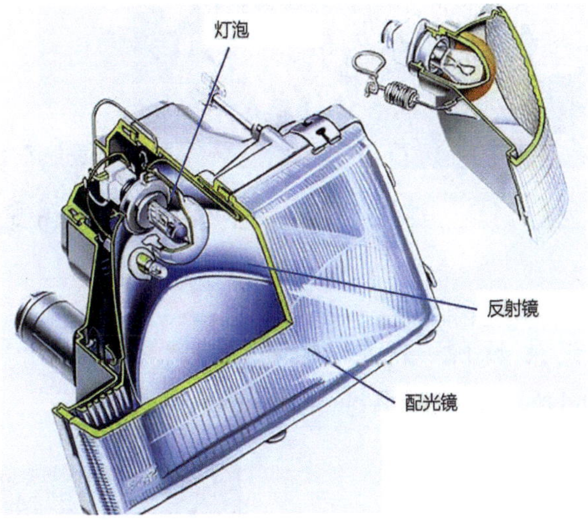

Qìchē qiánzhàodēng duì fāguāng qiángdù hé zhàoshè wèizhì de yāoqiú jiào gāo, yīncǐ xūyào tèshū
汽车前照灯对发光强度和照射位置的要求较高，因此需要特殊

de jiégòu shèjì. Qiánzhàodēng yóu
的结构设计。前照灯由（1）________________、（2）________________

hé dēngpào zǔchéng. Fǎnshèjìng de zuòyòng shì jiāng fāchū de guāng
和灯泡组成。反射镜的作用是将（3）________________发出的光

jùchéng qiángguāngshù, zēngjiā zhàoshè jùlí. Pèiguāngjìng de zuòyòng shì jiāng fǎnshè guāngshù kuòsàn
聚成强光束，增加照射距离。配光镜的作用是将反射光束扩散

fēnpèi, shǐ lùmiàn zhàomíng gèngjiā jūnyún.
分配，使路面照明更加均匀。

Automobile headlamps have high requirements for luminous intensity and irradiation position, thus requiring special structural design. The headlamp consists of a reflector, a lens and a bulb. The function of the reflector is to condense the light emitted by the bulb into a strong beam and increase the irradiation distance. The function of the lens is to diffuse and distribute the reflected beam to achieve more uniform road lighting.

2. 说一说 Let's talk

说说汽车前照灯的组成。**Talk about the components of an automobile headlamp.**

四、学以致用 xuéyǐzhìyòng Practicing What You Have Learnt

观看介绍前照灯故障诊断相关视频，了解前照灯故障诊断的步骤，然后将以下步骤排序。**Watch the related video introducing headlamp fault diagnosis, learn about the steps of headlamp fault diagnosis, and sort them out.**

dǎkāi dēngguāng kāiguān, jìlù gùzhàng xiànxiàng
A. 打开灯光开关，记录故障现象
turn on the light switch and record the fault phenomenon

shǐyòng wànyòngbiǎo jiǎncè
B. 使用万用表检测
detect it with a multimeter

liánjiē gùzhàng zhěnduànyí, chákàn gùzhàngmǎ
C. 连接故障诊断仪，查看故障码
connect the fault diagnosis instrument and check the fault code

xiūfù gùzhàng bìng yànzhèng
D. 修复故障并验证
remove and verify the fault

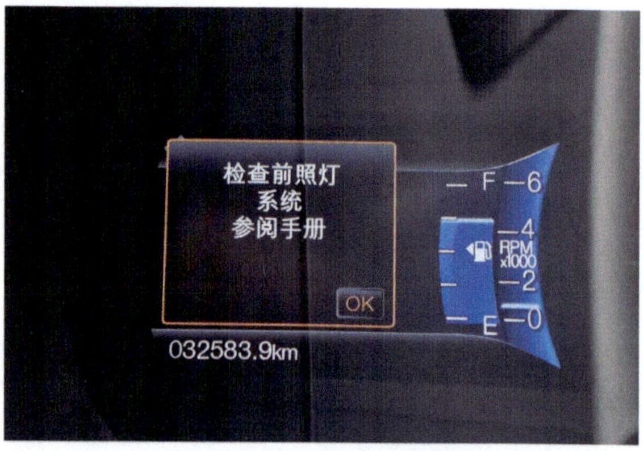

suǒdìng gùzhàngdiǎn
E. 锁定 故障点
locate the fault point

qīngchú gùzhàngmǎ hòu zàicì dúqǔ
F. 清除 故障码 后再次读取
clear the fault code and read it again

五、小知识 xiǎo zhīshi Tips

Qìchē qiánzhàodēng jìnhuàshǐ
汽车 前照灯 进化史

Suízhe 1885 nián Kǎ'ěr Běncí jiāng dì-yī tái qìchē dàidào rénlèi shēnbiān, qìchē qiánzhàodēng yě zài yì bǎi duō nián de lìshǐ zhōng búduàn jìnhuà. Dì-yī dài qiánzhàodēng shì yóu ránliào (làzhú、méiyóu huò yǐquē) zhíjiē ránshāo fāguāng, cúnzài fāguāng xiàolǜ dī、xìngnéng bù wěndìng、cāozuò fùzá děng míngxiǎn quēdiǎn. Dì-èr dài qiánzhàodēng shì báichìdēng. Dì-sān dài qiánzhàodēng shì lǔsù dēngpào. Zuòwéi báichìdēng de yì zhǒng, lǔsù dēngpào zài báichìdēng de jīchǔ shang jìnxíngle gǎijìn, guāngyuán chuāntòuxìng gèng qiáng. Dì-sì dài qiánzhàodēng shì xiānqì qiánzhàodēng, jùyǒu gāo fāguāng xiàolǜ、gāo liàngdù hé gāo kěkàoxìng děng yōudiǎn. Dì-wǔ dài qiánzhàodēng shì LED qiánzhàodēng, yě jiù shì bàndǎotǐ fāguāng èrjíguǎn. Dì-liù dài qiánzhàodēng shì jīguāng qiánzhàodēng. 2014 nián de Běijīng chēzhǎn, Bǎomǎ zài i8 chāojí pǎochē shang yùnyòngle jīguāng qiánzhàodēng.

随着1885年卡尔·本茨将第一台汽车带到人类身边，汽车前照灯也在一百多年的历史中不断进化。第一代前照灯是由燃料（蜡烛、煤油或乙炔）直接燃烧发光，存在发光效率低、性能不稳定、操作复杂等明显缺点。第二代前照灯是白炽灯。第三代前照灯是卤素灯泡。作为白炽灯的一种，卤素灯泡在白炽灯的基础上进行了改进，光源穿透性更强。第四代前照灯是氙气前照灯，具有高发光效率、高亮度和高可靠性等优点。第五代前照灯是LED前照灯，也就是半导体发光二极管。第六代前照灯是激光前照灯。2014年的北京车展，宝马在i8超级跑车上运用了激光前照灯。

Evolution History of Automobile Headlamps

With Carl Benz bringing the first automobile to mankind in 1885, automobile headlamps have been evolving endlessly for more than 100 years. The first-generation headlamps emitted light by directly burning fuel (candles, kerosene or acetylene) had obvious drawbacks such as low luminous efficiency, unstable performance and complex operation. The second-generation headlamps were incandescent lamps. The third-generation headlamps were halogen bulbs. As a kind of incandescent lamp, the halogen bulb has been improved on the basis of the incandescent lamp with stronger light source penetrability. The fourth-generation headlamps were xenon headlamps, with advantages of high luminous efficiency, high brightness and high reliability, etc. The fifth-generation headlamps were LED headlamps, that is, semiconductor light-emitting diodes. The sixth-generation headlamps were laser headlamps. At Auto China 2014, laser headlamps were adopted in BMW i8 supercars.

dì-yī dài ránliàodēng
第一代 燃料灯
the first-generation fuel lamp

dì-èr dài báichìdēng
第二代 白炽灯
the second-gereration incandescent lamp

dì-sān dài lǔsùdēng
第三代 卤素灯
the third-gereration halogen lamp

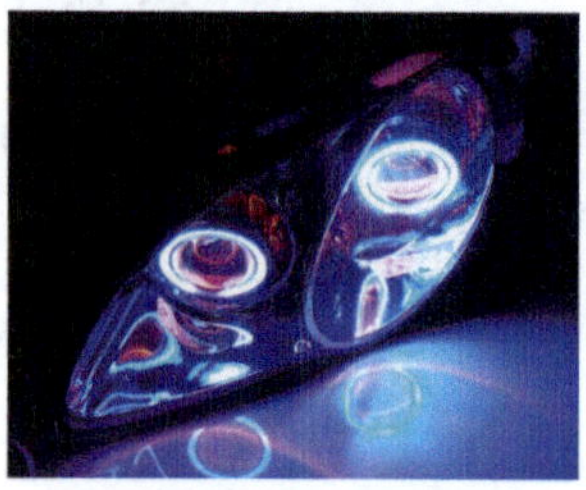

dì-sì dài xiāndēng
第四代 氙灯
the fourth-gereration xenon lamp

dì-wǔ dài LED dēng
第五代 LED 灯
the fifth-gereration LED lamp

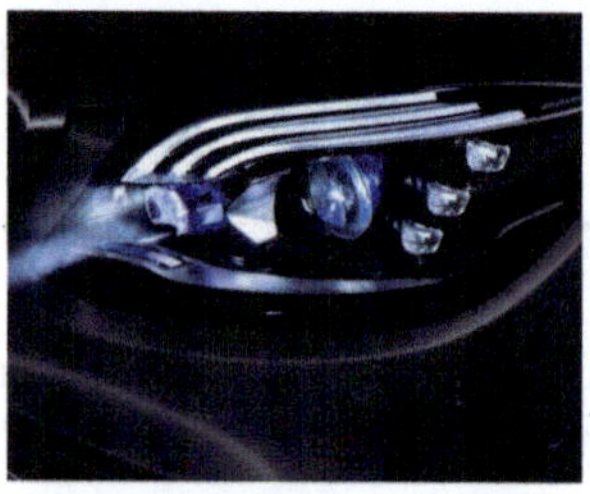

dì-liù dài jīguāngdēng
第六代 激光灯
the sixth-gereration laser lamp

补充专业词语 bǔchōng zhuānyè cíyǔ Supplementary Specialized Vocabulary

09-07

1.	反射镜	fǎnshèjìng	n.	reflector
2.	配光镜	pèiguāngjìng	n.	lens

3.	乙炔	yǐquē	n.	acetylene
4.	白炽灯	báichìdēng	n.	incandescent lamp
5.	卤素灯泡	lǔsù dēngpào	phr.	halogen bulb
6.	氙气前照灯	xiānqì qiánzhàodēng	phr.	xenon lamp
7.	半导体	bàndǎotǐ	n.	semiconductor
8.	发光二极管	fāguāng èrjíguǎn	phr.	light-emitting diode
9.	激光	jīguāng	n.	laser
10.	车展	chēzhǎn	n.	auto show
11.	超级跑车	chāojí pǎochē	phr.	supercar

第二部分 Part 2

汉字 Chinese Characters

一、汉字知识 Hànzì zhīshi Knowledge about Chinese Characters

汉字的偏旁（9） **Radicals of Chinese characters (9)**

偏旁 Radicals	例字 Examples	部件组合 Combinations	结构图示 Illustrations
耳	聊	耳＋卯	⿰
	职	耳＋只	⿰
	取	耳＋又	⿰
	联	耳＋关	⿰
欠	歌	哥＋欠	⿰
	歉	兼＋欠	⿰
	欢	又＋欠	⿰
冫	冷	冫＋令	⿰
	准	冫＋隹	⿰
	次	冫＋欠	⿰
彳	行	彳＋亍	⿰
	得	彳＋㝵	⿰
	律	彳＋聿	⿰
	很	彳＋艮	⿰

二、汉字认读与书写 Hànzì rèndú yǔ shūxiě The Recognition and Writing of Chinese Characters

认读下列词语，并试着读写构成词语的汉字。

Recognize the following words, and try to read and write the Chinese characters forming these words.

并联　冷区　再次　准备　行驶

并				联				冷				区			
再				次				准				备			
行				驶											

第三部分 Part 3

日常用语 *Daily Expressions*

1. 我们很乐意帮忙。Wǒmen hěn lèyì bāngmáng. We are happy to be of help.
2. 我保证通力合作。Wǒ bǎozhèng tōnglì hézuò. I can assure you of our full cooperation.
3. 所有这些产品都是我们的畅销货。Suǒyǒu zhèxiē chǎnpǐn dōu shì wǒmen de chàngxiāohuò. All these articles are our bestsellers.

第四部分 Part 4

单元实训 *Unit Practical Training*

前照灯故障检测 Headlamp Fault Detection

实训目的：Training purpose

通过本次实训，实训人员能够熟悉前照灯故障检测的一般步骤。

Through the practical training, the trainees will be able to be familiar with the general steps of headlamp fault detection.

实训步骤：Training steps

1. 教师准备前照灯有故障的车辆与相关检测工具。
   The teacher prepares vehicles with headlamp faults and related detection tools.
2. 教师讲解并演示前照灯故障检测的一般步骤。
   The teacher explains and demonstrates the general steps of headlamp fault detection.
3. 学员分组，每组 3 ～ 5 人。
   Divide the trainees into groups of 3-5.
4. 学员正确使用工具，检测前照灯的故障，修复故障并进行验证。
   The trainees use tools correctly to detect headlamp faults, repair and verify the faults.

❺ 小组讨论，编写报告。

Carry out a group discussion and write a report.

❻ 教师总结评价，实训结束。

The teacher summarizes and evaluates, and the training ends.

第五部分 Part 5

单元小结 Unit Summary

cíyǔ
词语
Vocabulary

普通词语 General Vocabulary

1.	大致	dàzhì	adj.	general
2.	反映	fǎnyìng	v.	report, make known
3.	亮	liàng	adj.	bright
4.	原因	yuányīn	n.	reason
5.	没问题	méi wèntí	phr.	no problem
6.	稍后	shāohòu	adv.	later
7.	处理	chǔlǐ	v.	deal with
8.	确实	quèshí	adv.	indeed
9.	应该	yīnggāi	aux.	should
10.	恢复	huīfù	v.	return to normal

专业词语 Specialized Vocabulary

1.	近光灯	jìnguāngdēng	n.	low beam
2.	开关	kāiguān	n.	switch
3.	亮度	liàngdù	n.	brightness
4.	远光灯	yuǎnguāng-dēng	n.	high beam
5.	电源	diànyuán	n.	power supply
6.	控制器	kòngzhìqì	n.	controller
7.	灯泡	dēngpào	n.	bulb
8.	电阻	diànzǔ	n.	resistance, resistor
9.	无穷大	wúqióngdà	n.	infinity

cíyǔ
词语
Vocabulary

补充专业词语 Supplementary Specialized Vocabulary

1.	反射镜	fǎnshèjìng	n.	reflector
2.	配光镜	pèiguāngjìng	n.	lens
3.	乙炔	yǐquē	n.	acetylene
4.	白炽灯	báichìdēng	n.	incandescent lamp
5.	卤素灯泡	lǔsù dēngpào	phr.	halogen bulb
6.	氙气前照灯	xiānqì qiánzhàodēng	phr.	xenon lamp
7.	半导体	bàndǎotǐ	n.	semiconductor
8.	发光二极管	fāguāng èrjíguǎn	phr.	light-emitting diode
9.	激光	jīguāng	n.	laser
10.	车展	chēzhǎn	n.	auto show
11.	超级跑车	chāojí pǎochē	phr.	supercar

jùzi
句子
Sentences

1. 客户反映打开近光灯开关，左右亮度一样，但是打开远光灯开关，右边没有左边亮。
2. 麻烦你检测一下儿具体原因，帮客户修好。
3. 左、右近光灯正常，说明电源、控制器和开关都没有问题。那故障点可能在哪里？
4. 你把万用表拿过来，先测量右前远光灯的保险丝电阻。
5. 那就是保险丝坏了，导致系统断路。更换新的保险丝，应该会恢复正常。

10

Èrshǒuchē jiǎncè

二手车检测

Used Car Detection

èrshǒuchē jiǎncè bùzhòu

二手车检测 步骤

Steps of Used Car Detection

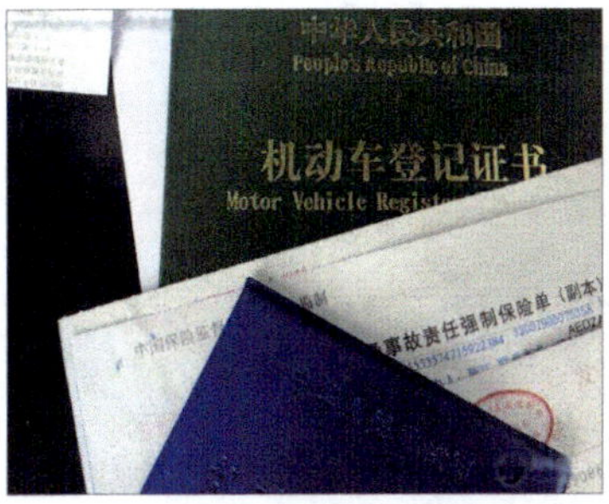

chēliàng shǒuxù jiǎnchá

车辆 手续 检查

Vehicle Formalities Check

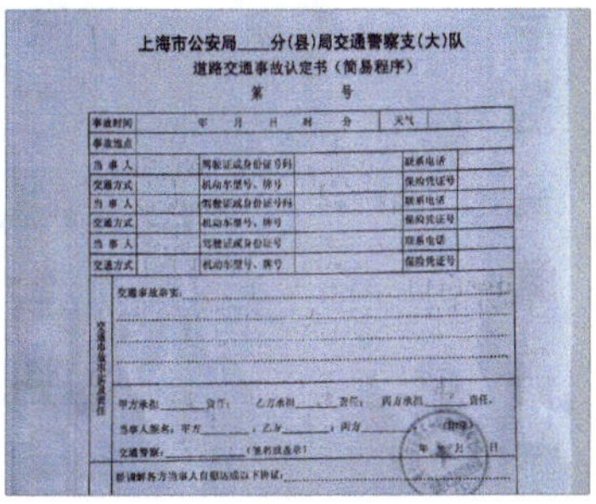
上海市公安局____分(县)局交通警察支(大)队

道路交通事故认定书（简易程序）

chēliàng shìgù jiàndìng

车辆事故鉴定

Vehicle Accident Identification

chēkuàng jiǎncè

车况 检测

Vehicle Condition Detection

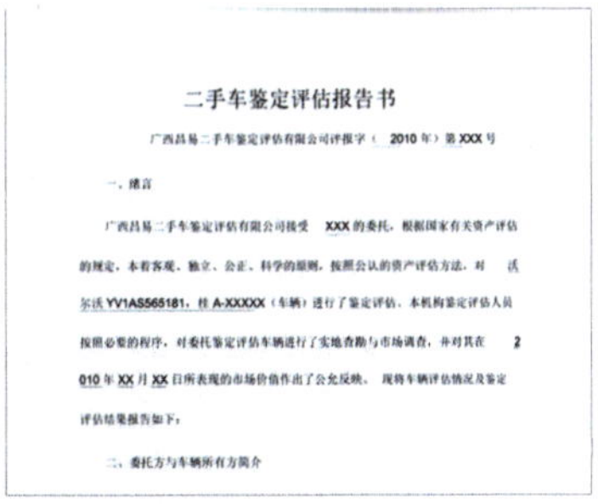
二手车鉴定评估报告书

chēkuàng píngjí

车况 评级

Vehicle Condition Rating

题解 Introduction

1. 学习内容：二手车检测的内容与流程，相关检测工具的使用。
   Learning content: The content and process of used car detection, and the use of relevant detection tools
2. 知识目标：学习二手车检测的关键词和常用句型，学习汉字的偏旁和结构，学写相关汉字。
   Knowledge objectives: To learn the keywords and common sentence patterns for used car detection, learn the radicals and structures of Chinese characters, and learn to write the related Chinese characters
3. 技能目标：掌握二手车外观检测的操作方法。
   Skill objective: To master the operation method of used car appearance detection

第一部分 Part 1

课文 Texts

一、热身 rèshēn Warm-up

1. 下面是汽车覆盖件的示意图，请选择数字对应的覆盖件名称。**The following is a schematic diagram of the car covering parts. Please select the names of the covering parts corresponding to the numbers.**

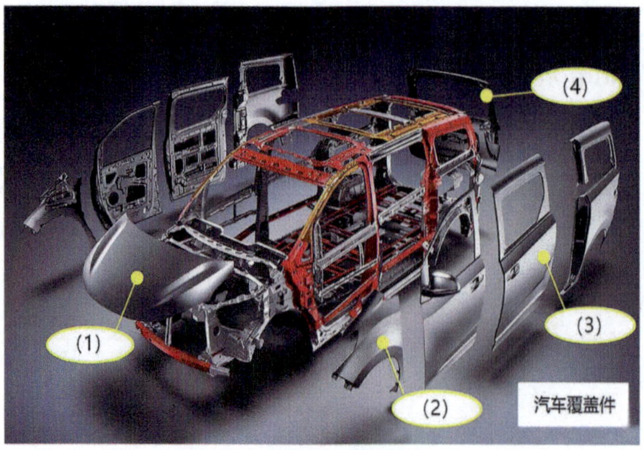

chēmén A. 车门 car door
yìzǐbǎn B. 翼子板 fender
hòubèixiāng gài C. 后备箱 盖 trunk lid
fādòngjīcāng gài D. 发动机舱 盖 engine compartment cover

(1)________ (2)________ (3)________ (4)________

2. 观看介绍汽车结构件相关视频，给图片中的结构件选择对应的名称。**Watch the related video introducing the automotive structural components and choose the corresponding names for the structural components in the picture.**

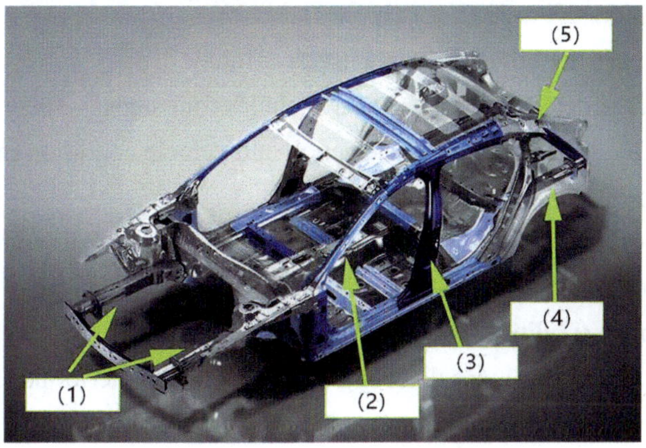

C zhù A. A柱 A-pillar
B zhù B. B柱 B-pillar
C zhù C. C柱 C-pillar
qiánzòngliáng D. 前纵梁 front longitudinal beam
hòuzòngliáng E. 后纵梁 rear longitudinal beam

(1)________ (2)________ (3)________ (4)________ (5)________

二、课文 kèwén Texts

A 10-01

túdi: Shīfu, jīntiān jiāo wǒ zěnme jiǎncè èrshǒuchē ba.
徒弟：师傅，今天教我怎么检测二手车吧。

shīfu: Yìbān lái shuō, èrshǒuchē jiǎncè fēnwéi sì gè bùzhòu: chēliàng shǒuxù jiǎnchá、chēliàng
师傅：一般来说，二手车检测分为四个步骤：车辆手续检查、车辆

shìgù jiàndìng、chēkuàng jiǎncè hé chēkuàng píngjí.
事故鉴定、车况检测和车况评级。

túdi: Shīfu, měi yí bù fēnbié xūyào zuò xiē shénme ne?
徒弟：师傅，每一步分别需要做些什么呢？

shīfu: Shǒuxiān yào héshí màifāng shēnfèn, cháyàn chēliàng xiāngguān shǒuxù jí zhēnwěi. Ránhòu zǐxì jiǎnchá, pànduàn chēliàng shìfǒu wéi shìgùchē huò pàoshuǐchē.
师傅：首先要核实卖方身份，查验车辆相关手续及真伪。然后仔细检查，判断车辆是否为事故车或泡水车。

túdi: Chēkuàng jiǎncè ne?
徒弟：车况检测呢？

shīfu: Chēkuàng jiǎncè bāokuò jiǎnchá wàiguān、nèishì hé qìchē sì dà bùjiàn děng, hái yào jìnxíng lùshì. Zuìhòu jìnxíng zǒngjié píngjí.
师傅：车况检测包括检查外观、内饰和汽车四大部件等，还要进行路试。最后进行总结评级。

译文 yìwén Text in English

Apprentice: Master, please teach me how to detect a used car today.

Master: Generally speaking, the detection of a used car includes four steps: vehicle formalities check, vehicle accident identification, vehicle condition detection and vehicle condition rating.

Apprentice: Master, what do I need to do for each step?

Master: First, verify the seller's identity, check the related formalities and their authenticity. Then inspect carefully to identify whether it is an accident car or a flood-damaged car.

Apprentice: What about vehicle condition detection?

Master: Vehicle condition detection includes detecting the appearance, interior parts and four major parts of the car. Also, conduct a road test. Finally, summarize and rate the car.

普通词语 pǔtōng cíyǔ General Vocabulary

10-02

1.	步骤	bùzhòu	n.	step
2.	手续	shǒuxù	n.	formalities
3.	评级	píngjí	v.	rate
4.	核实	héshí	v.	verify
5.	卖方	màifāng	n.	seller
6.	身份	shēnfèn	n.	identity
7.	查验	cháyàn	v.	check
8.	真伪	zhēnwěi	n.	authenticity

9.	仔细	zǐxì	adj.	careful
10.	总结	zǒngjié	v.	summarize

专业词语 zhuānyè cíyǔ Specialized Vocabulary

10-03

1.	二手车	èrshǒuchē	n.	used car
2.	事故	shìgù	n.	accident
3.	鉴定	jiàndìng	v.	identify
4.	车况	chēkuàng	n.	vehicle condition
5.	事故车	shìgùchē	n.	accident car
6.	泡水车	pàoshuǐchē	n.	flood-damaged car
7.	路试	lùshì	v.	road test

B 10-04

túdi: Shīfu, zěnme jiàndìng yí liàng chē shì bu shì shìgùchē huòzhě pàoshuǐchē ne?
徒弟：师傅，怎么鉴定一辆车是不是事故车或者泡水车呢？

shīfu: Wǒmen xiān lái huígù yíxiàr qìchē de jiégòu, chēshēn yǒu jiégòujiàn hé fùgàijiàn.
师傅：我们先来回顾一下儿汽车的结构，车身有结构件和覆盖件。

túdi: Shìde, shīfu.
徒弟：是的，师傅。

shīfu: Jiégòujiàn shòushāng zài xiūfù hòu de chē jiù jiào shìgùchē, cúnzài jiàshǐ ānquán yǐnhuàn.
师傅：结构件受伤再修复后的车就叫事故车，存在驾驶安全隐患。
Jiǎncè de shíhou yào zǐxì chákàn shìfǒu cúnzài zhězhòu hé qiēgē、hànjiē de hénjì.
检测的时候要仔细查看是否存在褶皱和切割、焊接的痕迹。

túdi: Nà pàoshuǐchē ne?
徒弟：那泡水车呢？

shīfu: Pàoshuǐchē, gùmíng-sīyì, shì zhǐ bèi shuǐ jìnpào guò de chēzi, tóngyàng wēixiǎn xìshù hěn gāo, róngyì duǎnlù、qǐhuǒ. Yào tèbié zhùyì chē shang de xiùjì hé fāméi de hénjì.
师傅：泡水车，顾名思义，是指被水浸泡过的车子，同样危险系数很高，容易短路、起火。要特别注意车上的锈迹和发霉的痕迹。

译文 yìwén Text in English

Apprentice: Master, how can we identify whether a car is an accident car or a flood-damaged car?

Master: Let's review the structure of a car first. The body has structural parts and covering parts.

Apprentice: Yes, master.

Master: An accident car is a car whose structural parts have been repaired after being damaged, which has potential driving safety hazards. During detection, carefully check whether there are wrinkles and cutting and welding marks.

Apprentice: What about a flood-damaged car?

Master: As the name suggests, a flood-damaged car refers to a car damaged by water. It also has a high hazard coefficient and is prone to short circuit and fire. We need to pay special attention to rust and mould stains on the car.

hànjiē hòu de jiégòujiàn
焊接后的结构件
welded structural parts

pàoshuǐchē
泡水车
flood-damaged car

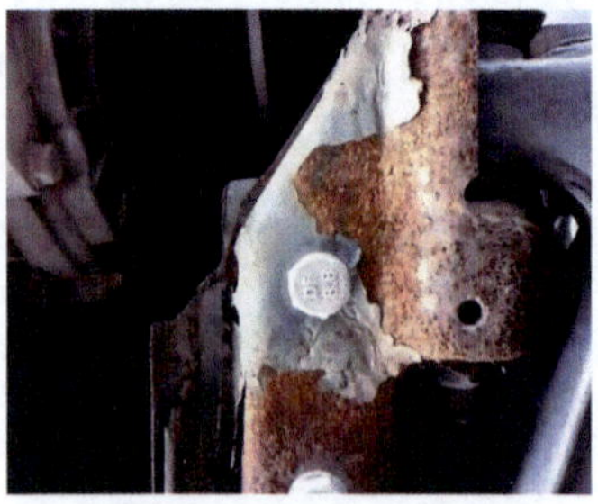

jīnshǔjiàn de xiùjì
金属件的锈迹
rust on metal parts

ānquándài fāméi
安全带发霉
mildewed seat belt

普通词语 pǔtōng cíyǔ General Vocabulary

10-05

1.	回顾	huígù	v.	review
2.	存在	cúnzài	v.	exist
3.	顾名思义	gùmíng-sīyì	phr.	as the name suggests
4.	浸泡	jìnpào	v.	soak
5.	特别	tèbié	adv.	especially

专业词语 zhuānyè cíyǔ Specialized Vocabulary

10-06

1.	结构	jiégòu	n.	structure
2.	结构件	jiégòujiàn	n.	structural part
3.	覆盖件	fùgàijiàn	n.	covering part
4.	褶皱	zhězhòu	n.	wrinkle
5.	切割	qiēgē	v.	cut
6.	焊接	hànjiē	v.	weld
7.	痕迹	hénjì	n.	mark, trace
8.	危险系数	wēixiǎn xìshù	phr.	hazard coefficient
9.	起火	qǐhuǒ	v.	(of a fire) break out
10.	锈迹	xiùjì	n.	rust
11.	发霉	fāméi	v.	mildew

三、视听说 shì-tīng-shuō Viewing, Listening and Speaking

1. 观看介绍二手车车身漆面检查相关视频，了解二手车车身漆面检查的方法，然后将以下图片与漆面检测方法配对。**Watch the related video introducing the inspection of the body paint surface of a used car, learn about the methods of inspecting the body paint surface of a used car, and then match the following pictures with the paint surface inspection methods.**

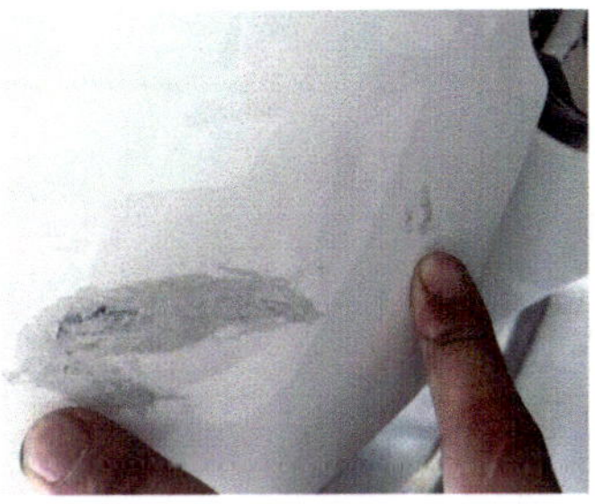

A.

B.

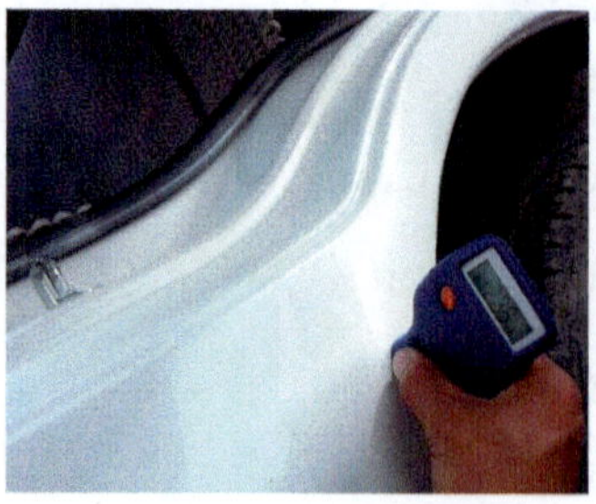

C.

D.

guānchá qīmiàn sèchā
❶ 观察 漆面色差 ________________
observe the color difference of the paint surface

shǐyòng qīmó jiǎncèyí jiǎncè
❷ 使用 漆膜检测仪检测 ________________
use a paint film detector for detection

shíbié fēi yóuqījiàn shang de pēnqī hénjì
❸ 识别非 油漆件 上 的喷漆痕迹 ________________
identify paint marks on non-painted parts

guānchá qīmiàn píngzhěngdù
❹ 观察 漆面 平整度 ________________
observe the smoothness of the paint surface

2. 说一说 **Let's talk**

说说漆面检测的方法。**Talk about the methods of paint surface inspection.**

四、学以致用 xuéyǐzhìyòng Practicing What You Have Learnt

观看介绍二手车车室检查相关视频，了解二手车车室检查的内容，然后将检查内容与图片配对。

Watch the related video introducing the interior inspection of a used car, learn about the contents of it, and then match the contents of the inspection with the pictures.

A.

B.

C.

D.

E.

zuòyǐ、 nèishì
① 座椅、内饰 seats, interior parts ____________

kāiguān ànniǔ
② 开关按钮 switch button ____________

yíbiǎo xìnxī
③ 仪表信息 dashboard information ____________

ānquán qìnáng
④ 安全气囊 airbag ____________

五、小知识 xiǎo zhīshi Tips

Èrshǒuchē lùshì yào jiǎnchá shénme
二手车路试要检查什么？

Tiāoxuǎn èrshǒuchē shí, lùshì shì bì bù kě shǎo de huánjié. Lùshì bú shì jiǎndān de "pǎo yì quānr", shì chē qián hòu dōu yīnggāi zǐxì jiǎnchá.
挑选二手车时，路试是必不可少的环节。路试不是简单的"跑一圈儿"，试车前后都应该仔细检查。

Lùshì qián yīng jiǎnchá fādòngjī qǐdòng、 dàisù shìfǒu yǒu yìxiǎng, wěiqì yánsè shìfǒu zhèngcháng. Zhèngcháng qíngkuàng xià, fādòngjī yīng zài sān cì nèi chénggōng qǐdòng, shēngyīn píngwěn yǒu jiézòu, páichū wúsè qìtǐ. Lùshì guòchéng zhōng yīng zhòngdiǎn jiǎnchá qǐbù、
路试前应检查发动机起动、怠速是否有异响，尾气颜色是否正常。正常情况下，发动机应在三次内成功起动，声音平稳有节奏，排出无色气体。路试过程中应重点检查起步、

jiāsù、 zhuǎnwān、jiǎnsù、 zhìdòng zhùchē děng shìfǒu zhèngcháng. Tóngshí yào jiǎnchá diànqì、
加速、转弯、减速、制动、驻车等是否正常。同时要检查电器、

sì mén chēchuāng shēngjiàng hé kōngtiáo xìtǒng xiàoguǒ. Lùshì hòu yào jiǎnchá yóuwēn、 lěngquèyè
四门车窗升降和空调系统效果。路试后要检查油温、冷却液

wēndù shìfǒu zài hélǐ fànwéi nèi, jiǎnchá chēliàng shìfǒu yǒu "sì lòu" qíngkuàng, jí shìfǒu
温度是否在合理范围内，检查车辆是否有“四漏”情况，即是否

cúnzài lòu shuǐ、 lòu yóu、 lòu qì hé lòu diàn de xiànxiàng.
存在漏水、漏油、漏气和漏电的现象。

What Should Be Checked for a Used Car Road Test?

When selecting a used car, road test is an essential part. It is not simply "to drive around". The car should be checked carefully before and after the test drive.

Before the road test, check whether the engine starts and idles with abnormal noise and whether the exhaust color is normal. In normal conditions, the engine shall be started successfully within three times with stable and rhythmic sound and discharge colorless gas. During the road test, check whether the starting, acceleration, turning, deceleration, braking, parking and other conditions are normal. At the same time, check the electrical appliances, the four car doors and windows and the effectiveness of the air conditioning system. After the road test, check whether the oil temperature and coolant temperature are within the reasonable range. Check whether the vehicle has "four leaks", that is, whether there is water leakage, oil leakage, gas leakage and electric leakage.

fādòngjī yìxiǎng
发动机异响
abnormal engine sound

páiqì yìcháng
排气异常
abnormal exhaustion

jiāsù nénglì chà
加速能力差
poor acceleration performance

lòu yóu
漏油
oil leakage

补充专业词语 bǔchōng zhuānyè cíyǔ Supplementary Specialized Vocabulary

10-07

1.	前纵梁	qiánzòngliáng	n.	front longitudinal beam
2.	后纵梁	hòuzòngliáng	n.	rear longitudinal beam

3.	漆面	qīmiàn	n.	paint surface
4.	漆膜检测仪	qīmó jiǎncèyí	phr.	paint film thickness detector
5.	异响	yìxiǎng	n.	abnormal sound

第二部分 Part 2

汉字 Chinese Characters

一、汉字知识 Hànzì zhīshi Knowledge about Chinese Characters

汉字的偏旁（10） Radicals of Chinese characters (10)

偏旁 Radicals	例字 Examples	部件组合 Combinations	结构图示 Illustrations
穴	空	穴 + 工	
	突	穴 + 犬	
	穿	穴 + 牙	
田	男	田 + 力	
	累	田 + 糸	
	思	田 + 心	
	备	夂 + 田	
	留	卯 + 田	
力	加	力 + 口	
	动	云 + 力	
	努	奴 + 力	
牛	物	牛 + 勿	
	特	牛 + 寺	

二、汉字认读与书写 Hànzì rèndú yǔ shūxiě The Recognition and Writing of Chinese Characters

认读下列词语，并试着读写构成词语的汉字。

Recognize the following words, and try to read and write the Chinese characters forming these words.

顾名思义　　特别　　空调　　起动　　制动

顾				名				思				义			
特				别				空				调			
起				动				制				动			

第三部分 Part 3

日常用语 Daily Expressions

1. 这是我们的共同愿望。Zhè shì wǒmen de gòngtóng yuànwàng. This is our common wish.
2. 百闻不如一见。Bǎi wén bùrú yí jiàn. Seeing is believing.
3. 英雄所见略同！ Yīngxióng suǒ jiàn lüè tóng! Great minds think alike!

第四部分 Part 4

单元实训 Unit Practical Training

二手车外观检测 Used Car Appearance Detection

实训目的 Training purpose

通过本次实训，实训人员能够掌握使用漆膜仪进行外观检测的方法。

Through the practical training, the trainees will be able to master the method of appearance detection with a paint film detector.

实训步骤 Training steps

1. 教师准备漆膜厚度检测仪、卷尺和实训车辆。

   The teacher prepares a paint film thickness detector, a tapeline and a training vehicle.

2. 教师讲解车辆外观的测量点，演示漆膜厚度检测仪的使用方法。

   The teacher explains the measurement points for the appearance of the vehicle and demonstrates the use of the paint film thickness detector.

   （1）机舱盖测量 5 处；

   Engine compartment cover: five points;

（2）前翼子板测量 6 处；

Front fender: six points;

（3）前车门测量 5 处；

Front car door: five points;

（4）后车门测量 5 处；

Rear car door: five points;

（5）后翼子板测量 5 处；

Rear fender: five points;

（6）后备箱盖测量 5 处；

Trunk lid: five points;

（7）车顶测量 9 处。

Car roof: nine points.

③ 学员分组，每组 4 人。

Divide the trainees into groups of four.

④ 学员检测，填写二手车外观鉴定作业表。

The trainees conduct the detection, and fill in the Used Car Appearance Appraisal Form.

⑤ 小组讨论，编写报告。

Carry out a group discussion and write a report.

⑥ 教师总结评价，实训结束。

The teacher summarizes and evaluates, and the training ends.

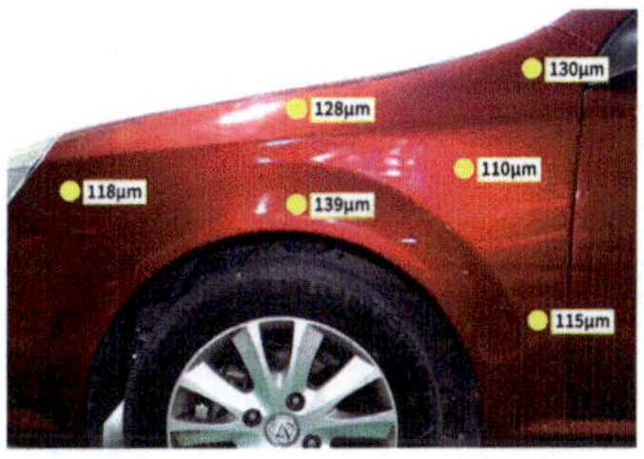

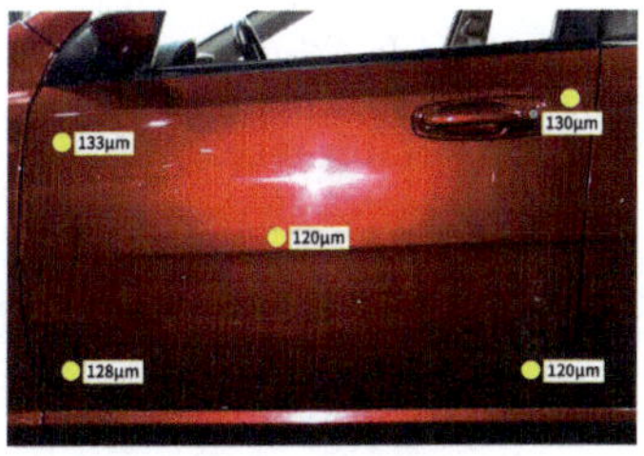

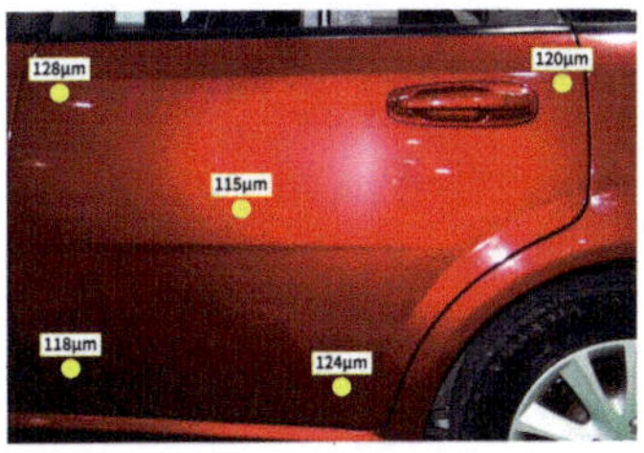

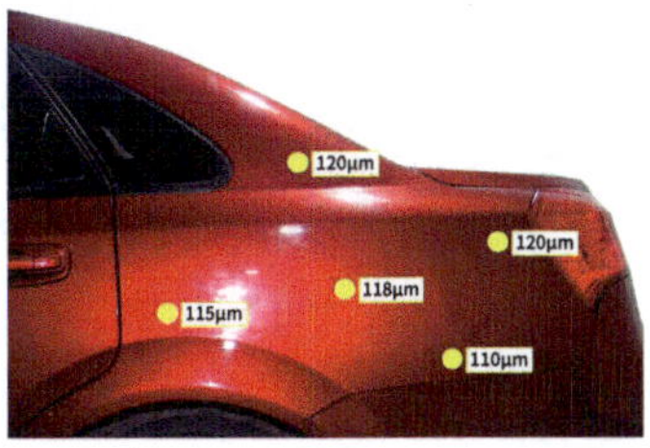

èrshǒuchē wàiguān jiàndìng zuòyèbiǎo 二手车 外观 鉴定 作业表 Used Car Appearance Appraisal Form		
jiàndìng nèiróng 鉴定 内容 Appraisal Content	xuǎnyòng gōngjù 选用 工具 Selected Tool	jiàndìng jiéguǒ 鉴定 结果 Appraisal Result
qián bǎoxiǎngàng lídì jiànxì 前 保险杠 离地间隙 Ground clearance of the front bumper	juǎnchǐ 卷尺 Tapeline	
hòu bǎoxiǎngàng lídì jiànxì 后 保险杠 离地间隙 Ground clearance of the rear bumper		
fādòngjīcāng gài 发动机舱盖 Engine compartment cover	qīmó hòudù jiǎncèyí 漆膜厚度检测仪 Paint film thickness detector	
zuǒ qián yìzǐbǎn 左 前 翼子板 Left front fender		
zuǒ qián chēmén 左 前 车门 Left front car door		
zuǒ hòu chēmén 左 后 车门 Left rear car door	qīmó hòudù jiǎncèyí 漆膜厚度检测仪 Paint film thickness detector	
zuǒ hòu yìzǐbǎn 左 后 翼子板 Left rear fender		
hòubèixiāng gài 后备箱 盖 Trunk lid		
yòu hòu yìzǐbǎn 右 后 翼子板 Right rear fender		
yòu hòu chēmén 右 后 车门 Right rear car door		
yòu qián chēmén 右 前 车门 Right front car door		

（续表）

èrshǒuchē wàiguān jiàndìng zuòyèbiǎo 二手车 外观 鉴定 作业表 Used Car Appearance Appraisal Form		
jiàndìng nèiróng 鉴定 内容 Appraisal Content	xuǎnyòng gōngjù 选用 工具 Selected Tool	jiàndìng jiéguǒ 鉴定 结果 Appraisal Result
yòu qián yìzǐbǎn 右 前 翼子板 Right front fender	qīmó hòudù jiǎncèyí 漆膜厚度检测仪 Paint film thickness detector	
chēdǐng 车顶 Car roof		

第五部分 Part 5

单元小结 Unit Summary

cíyǔ
词语
Vocabulary

普通词语 General Vocabulary

1.	步骤	bùzhòu	n.	step
2.	手续	shǒuxù	n.	formalities
3.	评级	píngjí	v.	rate
4.	核实	héshí	v.	verify
5.	卖方	màifāng	n.	seller
6.	身份	shēnfèn	n.	identity
7.	查验	cháyàn	v.	check
8.	真伪	zhēnwěi	n.	authenticity
9.	仔细	zǐxì	adj.	careful
10.	总结	zǒngjié	v.	summarize
11.	回顾	huígù	v.	review
12.	存在	cúnzài	v.	exist
13.	顾名思义	gùmíng-sīyì	phr.	as the name suggests
14.	浸泡	jìnpào	v.	soak
15.	特别	tèbié	adv.	especially

cíyǔ
词语
Vocabulary

专业词语 Specialized Vocabulary

1.	二手车	èrshǒuchē	n.	used car
2.	事故	shìgù	n.	accident
3.	鉴定	jiàndìng	v.	identify
4.	车况	chēkuàng	n.	vehicle condition
5.	事故车	shìgùchē	n.	accident car
6.	泡水车	pàoshuǐchē	n.	flood-damaged car
7.	路试	lùshì	v.	road test
8.	结构	jiégòu	n.	structure
9.	结构件	jiégòujiàn	n.	structural part
10.	覆盖件	fùgàijiàn	n.	covering part
11.	褶皱	zhězhòu	n.	wrinkle
12.	切割	qiēgē	v.	cut
13.	焊接	hànjiē	v.	weld
14.	痕迹	hénjì	n.	mark, trace
15.	危险系数	wēixiǎn xìshù	phr.	hazard coefficient
16.	起火	qǐhuǒ	v.	(of a fire) break out
17.	锈迹	xiùjì	n.	rust
18.	发霉	fāméi	v.	mildew

补充专业词语 Supplementary Specialized Vocabulary

1.	前纵梁	qiánzòngliáng	n.	front longitudinal beam
2.	后纵梁	hòuzòngliáng	n.	rear longitudinal beam
3.	漆面	qīmiàn	n.	paint surface
4.	漆膜检测仪	qīmó jiǎncèyí	phr.	paint film thickness detector
5.	异响	yìxiǎng	n.	abnormal sound

jùzi 句子 Sentences	1. 一般来说，二手车检测分为四个步骤：车辆手续检查、车辆事故鉴定、车况检测和车况评级。 2. 首先要核实卖方身份，查验车辆相关手续及真伪。然后仔细检查，判断车辆是否为事故车或泡水车。 3. 车况检测包括检查外观、内饰和汽车四大部件等，还要进行路试。最后进行总结评级。 4. 结构件受伤再修复后的车就叫事故车，存在驾驶安全隐患。检测的时候要仔细查看是否存在褶皱和切割、焊接的痕迹。 5. 泡水车，顾名思义，是指被水浸泡过的车子，同样危险系数很高，容易短路、起火。要特别注意车上的锈迹和发霉的痕迹。

附录　Appendixes

词汇总表　Vocabulary

序号	生词	拼音	词性	词义	普通 G 专业 S	所属单元
1	安装	ānzhuāng	v.	install	S	6B
2	凹槽	āocáo	n.	groove	S	6
3	白炽灯	báichìdēng	n.	incandescent lamp	S	9
4	半导体	bàndǎotǐ	n.	semiconductor	S	9
5	保持	bǎochí	v.	keep	G	4A
6	保险丝架	bǎoxiǎnsījià	n.	fuse holder	S	3A
7	报警灯	bàojǐngdēng	n.	alarm lamp	S	7
8	抱死	bàosǐ	v.	lock	S	8A
9	编号	biānhào	n.	serial number	G	3B
10	标注	biāozhù	v.	mark, label	G	3B
11	标准	biāozhǔn	n.	standard	S	2A
12	别的	biéde	pron.	other	G	2B
13	波形	bōxíng	n.	waveform	S	1B
14	不过	búguò	conj.	however	G	3A
15	补给	bǔjǐ	v.	supply	S	5
16	不停	bù tíng	phr.	constantly	G	2A
17	步骤	bùzhòu	n.	step	G	10A
18	采集	cǎijí	v.	collect	S	8B
19	采用	cǎiyòng	v.	adopt	S	1B
20	操作	cāozuò	v.	operate	S	4B
21	侧滑	cèhuá	v.	side skidding	S	8
22	插接器	chājiēqì	n.	plug connector	S	3A
23	查验	cháyàn	v.	check	G	10A
24	拆	chāi	v.	disassemble	S	2B
25	拆卸	chāixiè	v.	disassemble	S	5A
26	尝试	chángshì	v.	try	G	7A
27	常用	cháng yòng	phr.	frequently used	G	3B
28	厂商自定义接口	chǎngshāng zìdìngyì jiēkǒu	phr.	manufacturer's custom interface	S	1A
29	超级跑车	chāojí pǎochē	phr.	supercar	S	9
30	车况	chēkuàng	n.	vehicle condition	S	10A

（续表）

序号	生词	拼音	词性	词义	普通 G 专业 S	所属单元
31	车载电网控制单元	chēzài diànwǎng kòngzhì dānyuán	phr.	on-board supply control unit	S	3A
32	车展	chēzhǎn	n.	auto show	S	9
33	出	chū	v.	occur	G	1A
34	出现	chūxiàn	v.	appear	G	1B
35	初步	chūbù	adj.	preliminary	G	8A
36	处理	chǔlǐ	v.	deal with	G	9A
37	传输	chuánshū	v.	transmit	S	1B
38	磁性	cíxìng	n.	magnetism	S	4
39	此	cǐ	pron.	this	G	3B
40	此次	cǐ cì	phr.	this time	G	4A
41	存在	cúnzài	v.	exist	G	10B
42	搭铁	dātiě	v.	ground	S	3A
43	打滑	dǎhuá	v.	skid	S	8A
44	打紧	dǎjǐn	phr.	become tight	S	6B
45	大部分	dàbùfen	n.	most, majority	G	1B
46	大都	dàdū	adv.	mostly, mainly	G	1B
47	大致	dàzhì	adj.	general	G	9A
48	代码	dàimǎ	n.	code	S	3A
49	怠速	dàisù	v.	idle	S	7A
50	但	dàn	conj.	however	G	5B
51	导线编号	dǎoxiàn biānhào	phr.	wire number	S	3
52	导线颜色	dǎoxiàn yánsè	phr.	wire color	S	3
53	导致	dǎozhì	v.	result in, lead to	G	9B
54	到位	dàowèi	v.	be in place	G	7B
55	灯泡	dēngpào	n.	bulb	S	9B
56	低于	dīyú	phr.	be lower than, below	G	2A
57	滴	dī	v.	drip	G	4B
58	第二代车载诊断系统	dì-èr dài chēzài zhěnduàn xìtǒng	phr.	on-board diagnostics II (OBD-II)	S	1A
59	点火线圈	diǎnhuǒ xiànquān	phr.	ignition coil	S	3B
60	电控单元	diànkòng dānyuán	phr.	electronic control unit	S	3B
61	电控系统	diànkòng xìtǒng	phr.	electronic control system	S	7A
62	电量	diànliàng	n.	electric quantity	S	2

（续表）

序号	生词	拼音	词性	词义	普通 G 专业 S	所属单元
63	电源	diànyuán	n.	power supply	S	9B
64	电子控制	diànzǐ kòngzhì	phr.	electronic control	S	2
65	电子控制单元	diànzǐ kòngzhì dānyuán	phr.	electronic control unit	S	8
66	电阻	diànzǔ	n.	resistance, resistor	S	9B
67	定期保养	dìngqī bǎoyǎng	phr.	regular maintenance	S	4A
68	抖动	dǒudòng	v.	shake	S	7A
69	读取	dúqǔ	v.	read, get	G	1B
70	堵塞	dǔsè	v.	block	S	5B
71	端子	duānzǐ	n.	pin, stitch	S	1A
72	短路	duǎnlù	v.	short circuit	S	3A
73	断路	duànlù	v.	open circuit	S	3A
74	断线	duànxiàn	v.	breaka circuit	S	3B
75	对	duì	adj.	yes, right	G	3A
76	顿挫	dùncuò	v.	stumble	S	5B
77	二手车	èrshǒuchē	n.	used car	S	10A
78	发光二极管	fāguāng èrjíguǎn	phr.	light-emitting diode	S	9
79	发挥	fāhuī	v.	give play to	G	4A
80	发霉	fāméi	v.	mildew	S	10B
81	发现	fāxiàn	v.	find	G	2B
82	反射镜	fǎnshèjìng	n.	reflector	S	9
83	反应	fǎnyìng	n.	response	G	7B
84	反映	fǎnyìng	v.	report, make known	G	9A
85	防抱死制动系统	fángbàosǐ zhìdòng xìtǒng	phr.	anti-lock braking system	S	8A
86	防止	fángzhǐ	v.	prevent	G	4B
87	放油螺栓	fàngyóu luóshuān	phr.	oil drain bolt	S	4B
88	粉尘	fěnchén	n.	dust	S	5B
89	复查	fùchá	v.	recheck	S	6B
90	复原	fùyuán	v.	restore	S	7B
91	覆盖件	fùgàijiàn	n.	covering part	S	10B
92	干净	gānjìng	adj.	clean	G	4B
93	缸	gāng	n.	cylinder	S	7A
94	给	gěi	prep.	for	G	3B

（续表）

序号	生词	拼音	词性	词义	普通 G 专业 S	所属单元
95	更换	gēnghuàn	v.	replace	S	5A
96	公里	gōnglǐ	m.	kilometer	G	4A
97	固定	gùdìng	v.	fix	S	6B
98	固定螺丝	gùdìng luósī	phr.	fixing screw	S	5
99	故障灯	gùzhàngdēng	n.	fault light	S	8A
100	故障点	gùzhàngdiǎn	n.	fault point	S	7B
101	故障码	gùzhàngmǎ	n.	fault code	S	7A
102	顾名思义	gùmíng-sīyì	phr.	as the name suggests	G	10B
103	惯例	guànlì	n.	convention	G	7B
104	规定接口	guīdìng jiēkǒu	phr.	specified interface	S	1A
105	规定力矩	guīdìng lìjǔ	phr.	specified torque	S	4B
106	国际标准	guójì biāozhǔn	phr.	international standard	S	1A
107	果然	guǒrán	conj.	as expected	G	7A
108	过低	guò dī	phr.	too low	G	2A
109	过滤	guòlǜ	v.	filter	S	4A
110	还要	hái yào	phr.	still have to	G	5B
111	焊接	hànjiē	v.	weld	S	10B
112	行	háng	m.	line	G	3B
113	核实	héshí	v.	verify	G	10A
114	痕迹	hénjì	n.	mark, trace	S	10B
115	后纵梁	hòuzòngliáng	n.	rear longitudinal beam	S	10
116	缓慢	huǎnmàn	adj.	slow	S	5B
117	黄色	huángsè	n.	yellow	G	2A
118	灰尘	huīchén	n.	dust	G	5A
119	恢复	huīfù	v.	return to normal	G	9B
120	回顾	huígù	v.	review	G	10B
121	会	huì	aux.	may, can	G	5B
122	机械运动	jīxiè yùndòng	phr.	mechanical motion	S	2
123	机油回收机	jīyóu huíshōujī	phr.	oil recycling machine	S	4B
124	激光	jīguāng	n.	laser	S	9
125	极限标志	jíxiàn biāozhì	phr.	limit mark	S	6
126	急加速	jí jiāsù	phr.	rapid acceleration	S	5B
127	加油站	jiāyóuzhàn	n.	gas station	S	5B

（续表）

序号	生词	拼音	词性	词义	普通 G 专业 S	所属单元
128	加注	jiāzhù	v.	fill	S	4B
129	加注口盖	jiāzhùkǒugài	n.	filler cap	S	4
130	监测	jiāncè	v.	monitor	S	2A
131	检修	jiǎnxiū	v.	overhaul	S	2B
132	简单	jiǎndān	adj.	simple	G	3B
133	间接式	jiànjiēshì	adj.	indirect-type	S	2A
134	鉴定	jiàndìng	v.	identify	S	10A
135	讲	jiǎng	v.	tell	G	3B
136	胶质	jiāozhì	n.	colloid	S	5B
137	轿车	jiàochē	n.	sedan	S	8
138	接口	jiēkǒu	n.	interface	S	1A
139	接入	jiērù	v.	access	S	1A
140	结构	jiégòu	n.	structure	S	10B
141	结构件	jiégòujiàn	n.	structural part	S	10B
142	结合	jiéhé	v.	combine	G	7B
143	解除	jiěchú	v.	remove	S	7B
144	紧固	jǐngù	v.	tighten	S	6B
145	紧急	jǐnjí	adj.	urgent	G	8A
146	进气管	jìnqìguǎn	n.	intake pipe	S	5A
147	进气温度传感器	jìnqì wēndù chuángǎnqì	phr.	intake air temperature sensor	S	2B
148	近光灯	jìnguāngdēng	n.	low beam	S	9A
149	浸泡	jìnpào	v.	soak	G	10B
150	经过	jīngguò	v.	go through	G	5B
151	旧	jiù	adj.	old	G	4B
152	据说	jùshuō	v.	it is said	G	4A
153	开关	kāiguān	n.	switch	S	9A
154	看懂	kàndǒng	phr.	understand	G	3A
155	看起来	kàn qilai	phr.	look	G	5B
156	颗粒	kēlì	n.	particle	S	5B
157	壳	ké	n.	housing	S	5A
158	刻度尺	kèdùchǐ	n.	scale	S	4
159	控制器	kòngzhìqì	n.	controller	S	9B

（续表）

序号	生词	拼音	词性	词义	普通 G 专业 S	所属单元
160	控制器局域网络	kòngzhìqì júyù wǎngluò	phr.	Controller Area Network (CAN)	S	1B
161	拉起	lāqǐ	phr.	pull	G	6A
162	蓝牙模块	lányá mókuài	phr.	bluetooth module	S	1A
163	类型	lèixíng	n.	type	G	2B
164	冷却液	lěngquèyè	n.	coolant	S	2B
165	冷却液道	lěngquèyèdào	n.	coolant pipeline	S	2B
166	冷却液温度传感器	lěngquèyè wēndù chuángǎnqì	phr.	coolant temperature sensor	S	2B
167	历史	lìshǐ	n.	one's past/record	G	8B
168	例如	lìrú	v.	take for example	G	2B
169	连接	liánjiē	v.	connect	S	3B
170	亮	liàng	adj.	bright	G	9A
171	亮度	liàngdù	n.	brightness	S	9A
172	零件	língjiàn	n.	spare part(s)	S	7A
173	另	lìng	pron.	another	G	3B
174	另外	lìngwài	conj.	in addition	G	3B
175	漏气	lòu qì	phr.	leak air	S	2A
176	卤素灯泡	lǔsù dēngpào	phr.	halogen bulb	S	9
177	路试	lùshì	v.	road test	S	10A
178	滤布	lǜbù	n.	filter cloth	S	5A
179	滤芯	lǜxīn	n.	filter element	S	5A
180	轮速传感器	lúnsù chuángǎnqì	phr.	wheel speed sensor	S	8B
181	轮胎鼓包	lúntāi gǔ bāo	phr.	tire bulge	S	6
182	轮胎螺栓	lúntāi luóshuān	phr.	tire bolt	S	6A
183	轮胎压力传感器	lúntāi yālì chuángǎnqì	phr.	tire pressure sensor	S	2A
184	马上	mǎshàng	adv.	immediately	G	3A
185	卖方	màifāng	n.	seller	G	10A
186	没问题	méi wèntí	phr.	no problem	G	9A
187	每	měi	pron.	every	G	1A
188	密封圈	mìfēngquān	n.	seal ring	S	4
189	面积	miànjī	n.	area	G	5A
190	磨损	mósǔn	v.	wear (and tear)	S	5B

（续表）

序号	生词	拼音	词性	词义	普通 G 专业 S	所属单元
191	磨损标记	mósǔn biāojì	phr.	wear mark	S	6
192	拿	ná	v.	bring	G	1A
193	那就	nà jiù	phr.	then	G	7A
194	内置式	nèizhìshì	adj.	internal (type)	S	5
195	能否	néngfǒu	v.	*used to ask sb. politely to do sth.*	G	3B
196	能够	nénggòu	aux.	can, be able to	G	4A
197	扭力扳手	niǔlì bānshou	phr.	torque wrench	S	6A
198	排放	páifàng	v.	emit	S	7
199	排气温度传感器	páiqì wēndù chuángǎnqì	phr.	exhaust air temperature sensor	S	2B
200	判断	pànduàn	v.	judge, tell	G	1B
201	跑偏	pǎopiān	v.	deviate	S	8
202	泡水车	pàoshuǐchē	n.	flood-damaged car	S	10A
203	配光镜	pèiguāngjìng	n.	lens	S	9
204	喷溅	pēnjiàn	v.	splash	S	4B
205	喷射	pēnshè	v.	inject, spray	S	5B
206	喷油器	pēnyóuqì	n.	fuel injector	S	5B
207	评级	píngjí	v.	rate	G	10A
208	破损	pòsǔn	v.	damage	G	8B
209	漆面	qīmiàn	n.	paint surface	S	10
210	漆膜检测仪	qīmó jiǎncèyí	phr.	paint film thickness detector	S	10
211	其中	qízhōng	n.	inside	G	5B
212	起动	qǐdòng	v.	start	S	1B
213	起动机	qǐdòngjī	n.	starter	S	3A
214	起火	qǐhuǒ	v.	(of a fire) break out	S	10B
215	气缸	qìgāng	n.	cylinder	S	5A
216	前纵梁	qiánzòngliáng	n.	front longitudinal beam	S	10
217	切割	qiēgē	v.	cut	S	10B
218	清除	qīngchú	v.	clear	G	8B
219	清洁	qīngjié	adj.	clean	S	4A
220	取	qǔ	v.	remove	G	5A
221	全	quán	adj.	complete	G	3B
222	确保	quèbǎo	v.	ensure	G	8B

（续表）

序号	生词	拼音	词性	词义	普通 G 专业 S	所属单元
223	确实	quèshí	adv.	indeed	G	9B
224	然后	ránhòu	conj.	then	G	3A
225	热敏电阻式	rèmǐn diànzǔshì	phr.	thermistor-type	S	2B
226	容灰量	rónghuīliàng	n.	ash capacity	S	5A
227	肉眼	ròuyǎn	n.	naked eye	G	5B
228	如果	rúguǒ	conj.	if	G	1B
229	沙粒	shālì	n.	sand grain	G	5A
230	闪烁	shǎnshuò	v.	flash	S	2A
231	稍后	shāohòu	adv.	later	G	9A
232	稍微	shāowēi	adv.	slightly, a little	G	6B
233	身份	shēnfèn	n.	identity	G	10A
234	使	shǐ	v.	cause, make	G	5B
235	使用年限	shǐyòng niánxiàn	phr.	durable years	S	6
236	使用寿命	shǐyòng shòumìng	phr.	service life	S	4A
237	事故	shìgù	n.	accident	S	10A
238	事故车	shìgùchē	n.	accident car	S	10A
239	是否	shìfǒu	adv.	whether	G	2A
240	手册	shǒucè	n.	manual, handbook	G	4A
241	手续	shǒuxù	n.	formalities	G	10A
242	数据	shùjù	n.	data	S	1B
243	数字	shùzì	n.	number	G	2A
244	水分	shuǐfèn	n.	moisture	S	5B
245	顺序	shùnxù	n.	order, sequence	G	6A
246	松	sōng	v.	unscrew	G	4B
247	胎压监测系统	tāiyā jiāncè xìtǒng	phr.	tire pressure monitoring system	S	2A
248	胎压值	tāiyāzhí	n.	tire pressure value	S	2A
249	套筒扳手	tàotǒng bānshou	phr.	socket wrench	S	6A
250	特别	tèbié	adv.	especially	G	10B
251	提示	tíshì	v.	prompt	S	8A
252	挺	tǐng	adv.	quite	G	5B
253	通信	tōngxìn	v.	communicate	S	1B
254	通信电缆	tōngxìn diànlǎn	phr.	communication cable	S	1
255	通知	tōngzhī	v.	notify	G	4A

（续表）

序号	生词	拼音	词性	词义	普通 G 专业 S	所属单元
256	图标	túbiāo	n.	icon	G	2A
257	外置式	wàizhìshì	adj.	external (type)	S	5
258	危险系数	wēixiǎn xìshù	phr.	hazard coefficient	S	10B
259	稳	wěn	adj.	stable	G	1A
260	无法	wúfǎ	v.	be unable (to do sth.)	G	1B
261	无穷大	wúqióngdà	n.	infinity	S	9B
262	下面	xiàmiàn	n.	below	G	3B
263	氙气前照灯	xiānqì qiánzhàodēng	phr.	xenon lamp	S	9
264	显示	xiǎnshì	v.	show	G	2A
265	现象	xiànxiàng	n.	phenomenon	G	5B
266	线路	xiànlù	n.	circuit, line	S	3A
267	线圈	xiànquān	n.	coil	S	3B
268	相关	xiāngguān	v.	be related	G	7B
269	相同	xiāngtóng	adj.	same	G	1A
270	效果	xiàoguǒ	n.	effect	G	5A
271	新	xīn	adj.	new	G	7A
272	信号反射	xìnhào fǎnshè	phr.	signal reflection	S	1
273	信号控制线路	xìnhào kòngzhì xiànlù	phr.	signal control circuit	S	3A
274	信号喇叭继电器	xìnhào lǎba jìdiànqì	phr.	signal horn relay	S	3A
275	信息	xìnxī	n.	information	G	1B
276	形式	xíngshì	n.	form	G	3B
277	修复	xiūfù	v.	repair	S	7A
278	锈迹	xiùjì	n.	rust	S	10B
279	压力值	yālìzhí	n.	pressure value	S	2A
280	延长	yáncháng	v.	prolong	G	4A
281	钥匙	yàoshi	n.	key	G	7B
282	页	yè	n.	page	G	3B
283	液压控制单元	yèyā kòngzhì dānyuán	phr.	hydraulic control unit	S	8
284	一下儿	yíxiàr	q.	*used after a verb to indicate one action/attempt*	G	3A
285	乙炔	yǐquē	n.	acetylene	S	9
286	一些	yìxiē	q.	some, any	G	3B
287	异常	yìcháng	adj.	abnormal	S	2B

（续表）

序号	生词	拼音	词性	词义	普通 G 专业 S	所属单元
288	异响	yìxiǎng	n.	abnormal sound	S	10
289	因为	yīnwèi	conj.	because	G	3B
290	隐患	yǐnhuàn	n.	hidden danger	S	5
299	应	yīng	aux.	should	G	2B
301	应该	yīnggāi	aux.	should	G	9B
302	影响	yǐngxiǎng	n.	impact	G	5B
303	优质	yōuzhì	adj.	high-quality	S	5A
304	有些	yǒuxiē	pron.	some	G	3A
305	原	yuán	adj.	original	G	5A
306	原来	yuánlái	adj.	original	G	6B
307	原因	yuányīn	n.	reason	G	9A
308	远光灯	yuǎnguāngdēng	n.	high beam	S	9A
309	运行	yùnxíng	v.	run, oprate	S	1A
310	杂质	zázhì	n.	impurity	S	4A
312	再次	zàicì	adv.	again	G	8B
313	则	zé	conj.	*indicating cause and effect, condition and result, etc.*	G	2B
314	怎么	zěnme	pron.	how	G	1B
315	怎样	zěnyàng	pron.	how (about), what	G	5B
316	找出	zhǎochū	phr.	find	G	5A
317	找到	zhǎodào	phr.	find	G	3A
318	褶皱	zhězhòu	n.	wrinklc	S	10B
319	这个	zhège	pron.	this	G	1A
320	真伪	zhēnwěi	n.	authenticity	G	10A
321	诊断	zhěnduàn	v.	diagnose	S	1A
322	正反面	zhèng-fǎnmiàn	n.	front and back sides	S	5A
323	直接	zhíjiē	adj.	direct	G	2A
324	直接式	zhíjiēshì	adj.	direct-type	S	2A
325	指令	zhǐlìng	n.	instruction	S	8
326	指示灯	zhǐshìdēng	n.	indicator light	S	2A
327	制动压力调节器	zhìdòng yālì tiáojiéqì	phr.	brake pressure regulator	S	8
328	终端电阻	zhōngduān diànzǔ	phr.	terminal resistor	S	1
329	注意	zhùyì	v.	pay attention to	G	5A

（续表）

序号	生词	拼音	词性	词义	普通 G 专业 S	所属单元
330	驻车制动	zhùchē zhìdòng	phr.	parking brake	S	6A
331	专用扳手	zhuānyòng bānshou	phr.	special wrench	S	4
332	转	zhuàn	v.	rotate	G	3A
333	仔细	zǐxì	adj.	careful	G	10A
334	总结	zǒngjié	v.	summarize	G	10A
311	足量	zú liàng	phr.	sufficient	G	5A
335	最好	zuì hǎo	phr.	best	G	4A
336	左侧	zuǒcè	n.	left side	G	2A
337	左后轮胎	zuǒ hòu lúntāi	phr.	left rear tire	S	2A
338	左前车轮	zuǒ qián chēlún	phr.	left front wheel	S	6A

视频脚本
Video Scripts

第一单元　故障诊断仪功能

一、热身

OBD II 诊断接口有 16 个端子，其中：

1. 端子 1、3、8、11、12、13 为厂家自定义接口；
2. 端子 2 为 SAEJ1850 总线（+）、端子 10 为 SAEJ1850 总线（−）；
3. 端子 4 为车身搭铁；
4. 端子 5 为信号搭铁；
5. 端子 6 为 CAN-H、端子 14 为 CAN-L；
6. 端子 7 为 K-line、端子 15 为 L-line；
7. 端子 16 为常电。

三、视听说

故障诊断仪读取数据流的操作流程为：

1. 诊断仪连接与打开；
2. 查看车辆信息，并在菜单栏中选择车型；
3. 选择想要测试的电控系统，如发动机控制系统、自动变速器控制系统、ABS 系统、安全气囊等等；
4. 读取数据流；
5. 查看数据。

四、学以致用

正常会出现的波形；CAN-L 断路会出现的波形；CAN-H 断路会出现的波形；CAN-L 搭铁会出现的波形；CAN-H 搭铁会出现的波形；CAN-L 与 CAN-H 短路会出现的波形。

第二单元　车用传感器

一、热身

1. 中央信息显示器（可显示轮胎气压）；2. 右后轮胎压力传感器；3. 右前轮胎压力传感器；4. 左后轮胎压力传感器；5. 遥控信号接收器；6. 车身稳定控制系统（ESP）；7. 组合仪表；8. 左前轮胎压力传感器。

三、视听说

1. 车轮转速传感器；2. 横向加速度传感器；3. 转向角传感器；4. 偏转率传感器；5. 制动压力传感器。

四、学以致用

1. 节气门位置传感器；2. 进气压力温度传感器；3. 爆震传感器；4. 凸轴位置传感器；5. 相位传感器；6. 氧传感器；7. 温度传感器。

第三单元　电路图解读

一、热身

1. J413 信号喇叭继电器；2. J519 车载电网控制单元；3. SB 保险丝架 B；4. SC 保险丝架 C；5. T24b 24 芯插头连接。

三、视听说

2号、3号线束在此页表示不全，在另一页中还有连接，所以用断线的形式表示。

四、学以致用

电路图中，所有线束都是按照回路原则设计的，每个线路都可以形成一条回路。下面我们来看一下儿蓄电池给J623供电的电流走向吧。蓄电池→SB17→J623(T91/86端子)→J623(T91/1端子和T91/2端子)→72搭铁点接地。

第四单元　三滤更换（1）

一、热身

机油具有润滑、洁净、密封、减震、冷却、防锈的作用。

三、视听说

师傅：我们来更换机油滤清器。

学徒：好的，我用机油滤清器专用扳手把它拧松，并取下来了。

师傅：好，现在用发动机机油涂抹在新的机油滤清器的O型密封圈上。

学徒：这样做能起到更好的润滑和密封作用，是吧？

师傅：是的，现在把新的机油滤清器装上吧。

学徒：好的。

师傅：注意，与安装表面接触后，用机油滤清器专用扳手再把滤清器拧紧至3/4圈，拧紧力矩：15牛·米。

四、学以致用

师傅：现在可以给这辆车加注新机油了。

学徒：好的，我旋下机油加注口盖。

师傅：好，注入新机油，同时观察加油加注量。

学徒：根据机油刻度尺测量的液位，新机油已经添加到位。

师傅：好的，做好安装复位，机油及机油滤清器更换到此结束。

第五单元　三滤更换（2）

一、热身

新鲜空气经过空气滤清器过滤之后，进入进气歧管，分配到发动机各气缸燃烧室。气体是由进气门打开关闭控制的，哪个缸需要做功了，就进气，然后与喷油器喷到气缸内的汽油结合，在气缸燃烧室内由火花塞产生的电火花点燃它们，简称做功。单个气缸工作完成。一般四缸发动机按一定顺序进行点火做功。做功后产生的废气通过排气门打开进入排气歧管，废气在排到空气中之前要满足排放标准，所以设置催化转化器吸收有害气体。最后消声器就是最后一环，降低高温废气的排气噪声。

三、视听说

师傅：找出车辆汽油滤清器的位置，准备更换汽油滤清器。汽油滤清器分为内置式和外置式两种型式。内置式安装在汽油箱里面、汽油泵进油口之前，一般和汽油泵组合在一起；外置式一般安装在汽车底盘下面。

学徒：好的，我把固定螺丝和三个卡扣拆下来了。

师傅：好的，外置式汽油滤芯是有方向的，一般在上面有“IN”“OUT”或者“→”标志，千万不要上错了。

学徒：我已经把新的汽油滤清器更换完成了。

四、学以致用

师傅：现在打开发动机舱盖，确认空气滤清器壳位置。空气滤清器的具体位置可在车辆维修手册中确定；或可根据经验确定，一般位于发动机舱左侧。

学徒：好的，我已经找到了。

师傅：好，打开空气滤清器壳，取出空气滤芯。用干净棉纱布擦拭空气滤清器壳及下体内壁，将尘土清除。使用原汽车型号的新空气滤芯，将新的滤芯放入滤盒中。

学徒：好的，师傅，已经放好了。

师傅：装回空气滤清器壳，盖上发动机舱盖。工具复位，整理工位。

第六单元　轮胎更换

一、热身

徒弟：师傅，如何拆下轮胎总成？

师傅：轮胎拆除步骤是先将车停在合适位置，注意这时车轮不离地面。第二步是按照顺序拧松螺栓。然后，举升车辆，拧下螺栓，最后，取下左前轮。

三、试听说

徒弟：师傅，那又如何安装轮胎呢？

师傅：先把轮胎固定在原来的位置，再按照图片上的顺序拧上螺栓，配合举升机。使用套筒扳手按照顺序拧紧螺栓，然后使用扭矩扳手打紧到固定扭矩。拧紧螺栓后再进行一次复查。

四、学以致用

轮胎总成必须更换的原因是轮胎达到胎面磨损标记，或者轮胎鼓包了，还有就是轮胎到使用年限了。看下面的视频：

1. 小王发现他的汽车轮胎鼓起来了一个大包；
2. 小李的汽车是2020年购买的，她发现轮胎上的标记是2009年生产的，距离现在已经十多年了；
3. 轮胎的磨耗已经完全到达了胎面指示标记处。

第七单元　发动机电控系统检测

一、热身

发动机电子控制系统，简称电控系统，是通过对发动机点火、喷油、空燃比和尾气排放等进行控制，使发动机在最佳状态下工作，达到整车性能好、节约能源、降低尾气排放的目的。发动机电子控制系统主要包括：电控点火系统（ESA）、电控燃油喷射系统（EFI）、怠速控制系统（ISC）、自诊断与报警系统等。

三、视听说

顾客：您好，我车的仪表盘上的机油压力报警灯亮了，怎么办？

技师：别着急，我先用诊断仪检测一下儿。

学徒：师傅，给您。是什么问题呢？

技师：是机油压力报警器故障。我查了线路，没有问题，可能是本体故障，更换一个新件，试一下儿。

学徒：师傅，换了一个新件，故障解除了。

四、学以致用

学徒：师傅，车间有台车起动后仪表盘显示发动机转速为0.

师傅：先用诊断仪读一下儿故障码。

学徒：诊断仪显示故障为转速传感器线束开路。

师傅：检查一下儿G28发动机转速传感器相关线路。

学徒：是线束松动了，插紧之后故障消失了。

第八单元　ABS故障诊断

一、热身

汽车防抱死制动系统即ABS，ABS就是在制动过程中防止车轮被制动抱死。它能提高制动减速度、缩短制动距离，有效地提高汽车制动方向的稳定性和转向操纵能力，保证汽车的行驶安全。

三、视听说

汽车防抱死制动系统，通常由车轮速度传感器、液压控制单元和电子控制单元 ECU 等组成。轮速传感器用于检测车轮的转速，并提供信号给 ECU。ECU 用于接收信号，分析判断后输出控制指令给液压控制单元。液压控制单元用于接收 ECU 的指令，控制制动压力调节器进行压力调节。

四、学以致用

徒弟：师傅，一般情况下，应该怎么进行 ABS 故障检测？

师傅：第一步，是确认故障情况，进行初步检查；
第二步，利用故障诊断仪读取故障码，初步确定故障部位；
第三步，利用必要的工具对故障部位进行深入检查，排除故障；
第四步，排除故障后，别忘记清除故障码；
第五步，检查 ABS 故障指示灯状态，如仍点亮，需继续排除故障；
最后，当 ABS 故障指示灯不再点亮后，进行路试，确认 ABS 恢复正常。

第九单元　汽车前照灯检测

一、热身

前照灯检测是车辆安全检查的重要项目，一般来说，使用自动式前照灯检测仪检测前照灯的步骤如下：

1. 车辆沿引导线居中行驶至规定的检测距离处停止；
2. 置变速器于空挡，车辆电源处于充电状态，开启前照灯远光灯；
3. 检测软件发出指令，仪器测量远光灯发光强度及照射位置偏移值；
4. 转换为近光灯，仪器检测近光光束明暗截止线转角的照射位置偏移值。

三、视听说

汽车前照灯对发光强度和照射位置的要求很高，因此需要特殊的结构设计。前照灯由反射镜、配光镜和灯泡组成。反射镜的作用是将灯泡发出的光聚成强光束，增加照射距离；配光镜的作用是将反射光束扩散分配，使路面照明更加均匀。目前汽车上主要使用的灯泡有白炽灯泡、卤素灯泡和氙气前照灯。

四、学以致用

学徒：师傅，如果汽车前照灯右前远光位置不高，我们应该如何进行检修呢？

师傅：这是汽车照明系统最常见的故障之一。首先，打开灯光开关，记录故障现象。然后，连接故障诊断仪，查看是否存在灯光相关故障。第三步，根据故障现象锁定可能的故障点。记住，故障点包括开关、控制器、继电器、保险丝、灯泡和线束等。第四步，用万用表检测相关部件及线束。检测完成后，修复故障，验证灯光效果。最后，记得消除故障码后再次读取。

第十单元　二手车检测

一、热身

汽车结构件是指车体框架，可以理解为支撑汽车的骨骼，是安全的第一保障。汽车的结构件包括前纵梁、后纵梁、A 柱、B 柱和 C 柱。汽车结构件是一体的，一旦受到损坏，修复就需要经过切割或焊接。如此，汽车的安全系数就会大幅下降。

三、视听说

徒弟：师傅，二手车的外观应该如何进行检测？

师傅：二手车最直接的外观就是漆面。首先，可以直接观察漆面平整度，查看是否存在开裂、起泡、锈蚀、划伤、凹陷等问题；其次，观察漆面是否存在色差；另外，还可以识别非油漆件上的喷漆痕迹；最后，也使用厚度检测仪进行检测，补漆的地方漆膜厚，测量数据大。

四、学以致用

徒弟：师傅，二手的车内要检查哪些部件呢？

师傅：首先要检查座椅、内饰是否干净、整洁，有没有更换过或者拆装过，然后看各个开关按钮是否功能良好；还需要启动车辆，来检查有无故障灯亮起，查看行驶里程；最后，别忘了检查安全气囊有无更换的痕迹。

徒弟：好的，我记录下来了。

参考答案
Reference Answers

第一单元　故障诊断仪功能

一、热身

1.（1）A （2）C （3）D （4）B

2.（1）厂家自定义接口 1、3、8、11、12、13

（2）SAEJ1850 总线（+） 2 、SAEJ1850 总线（-） 10

（3）车身地 4

（4）信号地 5

（5）CAN-H 6 、CAN-L 14

（6）K-line 7 、L-line 15

（7）常电 16

三、视听说

1. B　2. A　3. E　4. D　5. C

四、学以致用

1. A　2. C　3. E　4. D　5. B　6. F

第二单元　车用传感器

一、热身

1.（1）D （2）A （3）C （4）B

2.（1）B （2）C （3）A （4）H （5）D （6）F （7）G （8）E

三、视听说

1. B　2. E　3. A　4. D　5. C

四、学以致用

1. G　2. D　3. A　4. F　5. B　6. C　7. E

第三单元　电路图解读

一、热身

1.（1）D （2）B （3）E （4）F （5）A （6）H （7）C （8）G

2.（1）B （2）C （3）A （4）D （5）E

三、视听说

此电路图中，属于断线的是②、③

四、学以致用

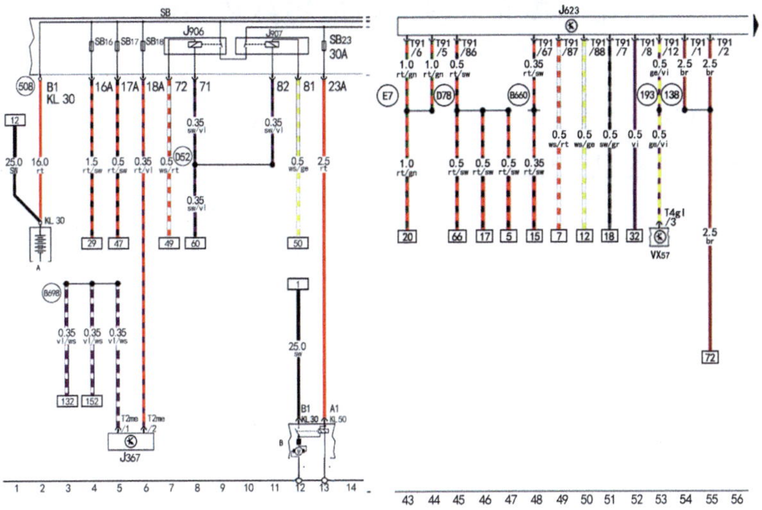

第四单元　三滤更换（1）

一、热身

1.（1）C　（2）A　（3）B　（4）D

2. A　B　C　E　H　I（排序不分先后）

三、视听说

1. B　2. D　3. A　4. C

四、学以致用

1. B　2. A　3. D　4. C

第五单元　三滤更换（2）

一、热身

1.（1）A　（2）C　（3）B

2.（1）A　（2）C　（3）B

三、视听说

1. C　2. A　3. B

四、学以致用

1. B　2. A　3. D　4. C

第六单元　轮胎更换

一、热身

1.（1）A　（2）D　（3）B　（4）C

2. B→C→A

三、视听说

C→A→B→E→D

四、学以致用

1. B　2. C　3. A

第七单元　发动机电控系统检测

一、热身

1.（1）C （2）D （3）A （4）B

2. 电控系统所控制的内容包括：A D E F

三、视听说

1. B　2. C　3. A

四、学以致用

1. C　2. A　3. D　4. B

第八单元　ABS 故障诊断

一、热身

1.（1）C （2）B （3）D （4）A

2. √ √ × √ √

三、视听说

（1）BF （2）AD （3）CE

四、学以致用

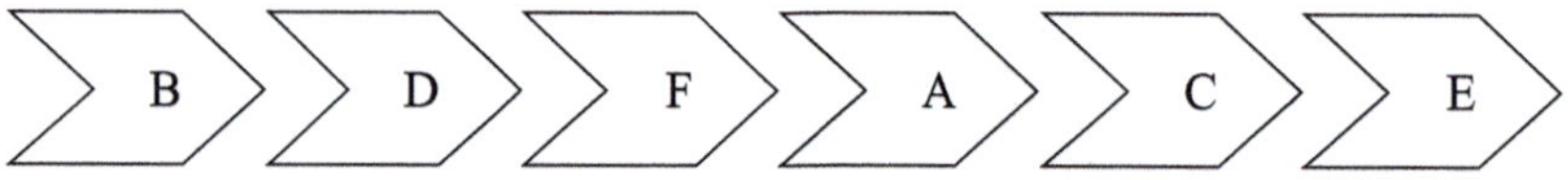

第九单元　汽车前照灯检测

一、热身

1.（1）C （2）B （3）D （4）E （5）A （6）F

2.

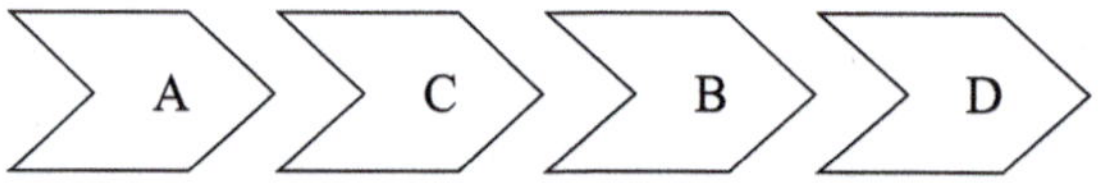

三、视听说

（1）反射镜 （2）配光镜 （3）灯泡

四、学以致用

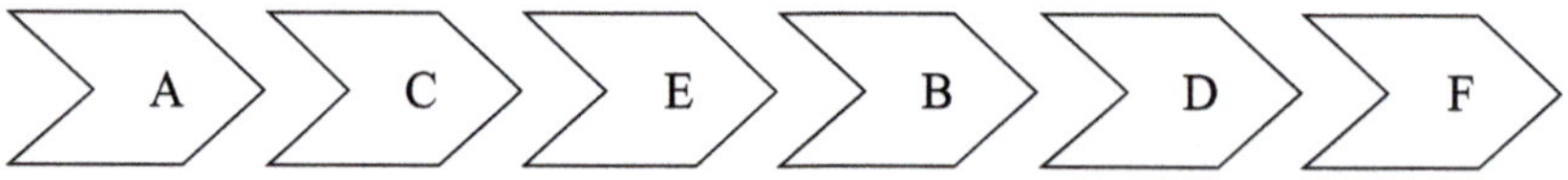

第十单元　二手车检测

一、热身

1.（1）D （2）B （3）A （4）C

2.（1）D （2）A （3）B （4）E （5）C

三、视听说

（1）B （2）C （3）A （4）D

四、学以致用

（1）A、D （2）E （3）B （4）C